The Orbis pictus of John Amos Comenius

Johann Amos Comenius

Editor: C. W. Bardeen

Alpha Editions

This edition published in 2019

ISBN : 9789353865344

Design and Setting By
Alpha Editions
email - alphaedis@gmail.com

As per information held with us this book is in Public Domain.
This book is a reproduction of an important historical work.
Alpha Editions uses the best technology to reproduce historical work in the same manner it was first published to preserve its original nature. Any marks or number seen are left intentionally to preserve its true form.

THE

ORBIS PICTUS

OF

JOHN AMOS COMENIUS.

This work is, indeed, the first children's picture book.—ENCYCLOPÆDIA BRITANNICA, 9TH EDITION, vi. 180.

SYRACUSE, N. Y.:
C. W. BARDEEN, PUBLISHER,
1887.

Copyright, 1887, by C. W. BARDEEN.

Olen
LT
101
C73
1887

6831 B 24

A.139122

G

It may not be generally known that Comenius was once solicited to become President of Harvard College. The following is a quotation from Vol. II, p. 14, of Cotton Mather's MAGNALIA:

"That brave old man, Johannes Amos Commenius, the fame of whose worth has been TRUMPETTED as far as more than three languages (whereof everyone is indebted unto his JANUA) could carry it, was indeed agreed withal, by one Mr. Winthrop in his travels through the LOW COUNTRIES, to come over to New England, and illuminate their Colledge and COUNTRY, in the quality of a President, which was now become vacant. But the solicitations of the Swedish Ambassador diverting him another way, that incomparable Moravian became not an American."

This was on the resignation of President Dunster, in 1654—NOTE OF PROF. PAYNE, COMPAYRE'S HISTORY OF EDUCATION, BOSTON, 1886, P. 125.

Family of S.G. Williams
6/7/900

Editor's Preface.

When it is remembered that this work is not only an educational classic of prime importance, but that it was the first picture-book ever made for children and was for a century the most popular text-book in Europe, and yet has been for many years unattainable on account of its rarity, the wonder is, not that it is reproduced now but that it has not been reproduced before. But the difficulty has been to find a satisfactory copy. Many as have been the editions, few copies have been preserved. It was a book children were fond of and wore out in turning the leaves over and over to see the pictures. Then as the old copper-plates became indistinct they were replaced by wood-engravings, of coarse execution, and often of changed treatment. Von Raumer complains that the edition of 1755 substitutes for the original cut of the Soul, (No. 43, as here given,) a picture of an eye, and in a table the figures I. I. II. I. I. II., and adds that it is difficult to recognize in this an expressive psychological symbol, and to explain it. In an edition I have, published in Vienna in 1779, this cut is omitted altogether, and indeed there are but 82 in place of the 157 found in earlier editions, the following, as numbered in this edition, being omitted:

1, the alphabet, 2, 36, 43, 45, 66, 68, 75, 76, 78–80, 87, 88, 92–122, 124, 126, 128, 130–141.

On the other hand, the Vienna edition contains a curious additional cut. It gives No. 4, the Heaven, practically as in this edition, but puts another cut under it in which the earth is revolving about the sun; and after the statement of Comenius, "*Coelum rotatur, et ambit terram, in medio stantem*" interpolates: "*prout veteres crediderunt; recentiores enim defendunt motum terrae circa solem*" [as the ancients used to think; for later authorities hold that the motion of the earth is about the sun.]

Two specimen pages from another edition are inserted in Payne's Compayré's History of Education (between pp. 126, 127). The cut is the representative of No. 103 in this edition, but those who compare them will see not only how much coarser is the execution of the wood-cut Prof. Payne has copied, but what liberties have been taken with with the design. The only change in the Latin text, however, is from *Designat Figuras rerum* in the original, to *Figuram rerum designat.*

In this edition the cuts are unusually clear copies of the copper-plates of the first edition of 1658, from which we have also taken the Latin text. The text for the English translation is from the English edition of 1727, in which for the first time the English words were so arranged as to stand opposite their Latin equivalents.

The cuts have been reproduced with great care by the photographic process. I thought best not to permit them to be retouched, preferring occasional indistinctness to modern tampering with the originals that would make them less authentic.

The English text is unchanged from that of the 1727 edition, except in rare instances where substitutions have been made for single words not now permissible. The typography suggests rather than imitates the quaintness of the original, and the paper was carefully selected to produce so far as practicable the impression of the old hand-presses.

In short my aim has been to put within the reach of teachers at a moderate price a satisfactory reproduction of this important book; and if the sale of the *Orbis Pictus* seems to warrant it, I hope subsequently to print as a companion volume the *Vestibulum* and *Janua* of the same author, of which I have choice copies.

C. W. BARDEEN.

Syracuse, Sept. 28, 1887.

Comments upon the Orbis Pictus.

During four years he here prosecuted his efforts in behalf of education with commendable success, and wrote, among other works, his celebrated Orbis Pictus, which has passed through a great many editions, and survived a multitude of imitations.—Smith's History of Education, N. Y., 1842, p. 129.

The most eminent educator of the seventeenth century, however, was John Amos Comenius......His Orbis Sensualium Pictus, published in 1657, enjoyed a still higher renown. The text was much the same with the Janua, being intended as a kind of elementary encyclopædia; but *it differed from all previous text-books*, in being illustrated with pictures, on copper and wood, of the various topics discussed in it. This book was universally popular. In those portions of Germany where the schools had been broken up by the "Thirty years' war," mothers taught their children from its pages. Corrected and amended by later editors, it continued for nearly two hundred years, to be a text-book of the German schools.—History and Progress of Education, by Philobiblius, N. Y., 1860, p. 210.

The "Janua" would, therefore, have had but a short-lived popularity with teachers, and a still shorter with learners, if Comenius had not carried out his principle of appealing to the senses, and called in the artist. The result was the "Orbis Pictus," a book which proved a favorite with young and old, and maintained its ground in many a school for more than a century.... I am sorry I cannot give a specimen of this celebrated book with its quaint pictures. The artist, of course, was wanting in the technical skill which is now commonly displayed even in the cheapest publications, but this renders his delineations none the less entertaining. As a picture of the life and manners of the seventeeth century, the work has great historical interest, which will, I hope, secure for it another English edition.—QUICK'S EDUCATIONAL REFORMERS, 1868; Syracuse edition, p. 79.

But the principle on which he most insisted is that the teaching of words and things must go together, hand in hand. When we consider how much time is spent over new languages, what waste of energy is lavished on mere preparation, how it takes so long to lay a foundation that there is no time to lay a building upon it, we must conclude that it is in the acceptance and development of this principle that the improvement of education will in the future consist. Any one who attempts to inculcate this great reform will find that its first principles are contained in the writings of Comenius.—ENCYCLOPAEDIA BRITANNICA, 9th edition, vii. 674.

The first edition of this celebrated book was published at Nuremberg in 1657; soon after a translation was made into English by Charles Hoole. The last English edition appeared in 1777, and this was reprinted in America in 1812. This was the first illustrated school-book, and was the first attempt at what now passes under the name of "object lessons." —SHORT HISTORY OF EDUCATION, W. H. PAYNE, Syracuse, 1881, p. 103.

Of these, the "Janua" and the "Orbis" were translated into most European and some of the Oriental languages. It is evident that these practices of Comenius contain the germs of things afterwards connected with the names of Pestalozzi and Stow. It also may be safely assumed that many methods that are now in practical use, were then not unknown to earliest teachers.—GILL'S SYSTEMS OF EDUCATION, London, 1876, p. 13.

The more we reflect on the method of Comenius, the more we shall see it is replete with suggestiveness, and we shall feel surprised that so much wisdom can have lain in the path of schoolmasters for two hundred and fifty years, and that they have never stooped to avail themselves of its treasures.—BROWNING'S INTRODUCTION TO THE HISTORY OF EDUCATIONAL THEORIES, 1882, New York edition, p. 67.

The "Orbis Pictus," the first practical application of the intuitive method, had an extraordinary success, and has served as a model for the innumerable illustrated books which for three centuries have invaded the schools.—COMPAYRE'S HISTORY OF PEDAGOGY, Payne's translation, Boston, 1886, p. 127.

He remained at Patak four years, which were characterized by surprising literary activity. During this short period he produced no less than fifteen different works, among them his "World Illustrated" *(Orbis Pictus)*, the most famous ot all his writings.

It admirably applied the principle that words and things should be learned together....The "World Illustrated" had an enormous circulation, and remained for a long time the most popular text-book in Europe.—PAINTER'S HISTORY OF EDUCATION, N.Y., 1886, p. 206.

Or, si ce livre n'est qu'un equivalent de la véritable intuition; si, ensuite, le contenu du tout paraît fort defectueux, au point de vue de la science de nos jours; si, enfin, un effort exagéré pour l' integrité de la conception de l' enfant a créé, pour les choses modernes, trop de dénominations latines qui paraissent douteuses, l' *Orbis pictus* était pourtant, pour son temps, une oeuvre très originale et très spirituelle, qui fit faire un grand progrés à la pedagogie et servit longtemps de livre d' ecole utile et de modèle á d' innomorables livres d' images, souvent pires.—HISTORIE D' ÉDUCATION, FREDERICK DITTES, Redolfi's French translation, Paris, 1880, p. 178.

Here Comenius wrote, among others, his second celebrated work the "Orbis Pictus." He was not, however, able to finish it in Hungary for want of a skilful engraver on copper. For such a one he carried it to Michael Endter, the bookseller at Nuremberg, but the engraving delayed the publication of the book for three years more. In 1657 Comenius expressed the hope that it would appear during the next autumn. With what great approbation the work was received at its first appearance, is shown by the fact that within two years, in 1659, Endter had published a second enlarged edition.—KARL VON

RAUMER, translated in Barnard's Journal of Education, v. 260.

The "Janua" had an enormous sale, and was published in many languages, but the editions and sale of the "Orbis Pictus" far exceeded those of the "Janua," and, indeed, for some time it was the most popular text-book in Europe, and deservedly so.—LAURIE'S JOHN AMOS COMENIUS, Boston edition, p. 185.

JOH. AMOS COMENII
Orbis Sensualium Pictus:

HOC EST

Omnium principalium in Mundo Rerum, & in Vita Actionum,

PICTURA & NOMENCLATURA.

JOH. AMOS COMENIUS's
VISIBLE WORLD:

OR, A

Nomenclature, and Pictures

OF ALL THE

CHIEF THINGS that are in the WORLD, and of MENS EMPLOYMENTS therein;

In above 150 COPPER CUTS.

WRITTEN

By the Author in Latin and High Dutch, being one of his last ESSAYS; and the most suitable to Childrens Capacity of any he hath hitherto made.

Translated into English

By CHARLES HOOLE, M. A.

For the Use of Young Latin Scholars.

The ELEVENTH EDITION Corrected, and the English made to answer Word for Word to the Latin.

Nihil est in intellectu, quod non prius fuit in sensu. Arist.

London; Printed for, and sold by *John* and *Benj. Sprint*, at the *Bell* in *Little Britain*, 1728.

Gen. ii. 19, 20.

The Lord God brought unto *Adam* every Beast of the Field, and every Fowl of the Air, to see what he would call them. And *Adam* gave Names to all Cattle, and to the Fowl of the Air, and to every Beast ot the Field.

Gen. ii. 19, 20.

Adduxit Dominus Deus ad Adam *cuncta Animantia Terræ, & universa volatilia Cœli, ut videret quomodo vocaret illa. Appellavitque* Adam *Nominibus suis cuncta Animantia, & universa volatilia Cœli, & omnes Bestias Agri.*

I. A. Comenii opera Didactica par. 1. p. 6, Amst. 1657. fol.

Didacticæ nostræ prora & puppis esto: Investigare, & invenire modum, quo Docentes minus doceant, Discentes vero plus discant: Scholæ minus habeant Strepitus, nauseæ, vani laboris; plus autem otii, deliciarum, solidique profectus: Respublica Christiana minus tenebrarum confusionis dissidiorum; plus lucis, ordinis, pacis & tranquilitatis.

The Author's Preface to the Reader.

Instruction is the means to expel Rudeness, with which young wits ought to be well furnished in Schools: But so, as that the teaching be 1. *True*, 2. *Full*, 3. *Clear*, and 4. *Solid*.

1. It will be *true*, if nothing be taught but such as is beneficial to ones life; lest there be a cause of complaining afterwards. We know not necessary things, because we have not learned things necessary.

2. It will be *full*, if the mind be polished for wisdom, the tongue for eloquence, and the hands for a neat way of living. This will be that *grace* of one's life, *to be wise*, *to act*, *to speak*.

3, 4. It will be *clear*, and by that, firm and *solid*, if whatever is taught and learned, be not obscure, or confused, but apparent, distinct, and articulate, as the fingers on the hands.

The ground of this business, is, that sensual objects may be rightly presented to the senses, for fear they may not be received. I say, and say it again aloud, that this last is the foundation of all the rest: because we can neither act nor speak wisely, unless we first rightly understand all the things which are to be done, and whereof we are to speak. Now there is nothing in the understanding, which was not before in the sense. And therefore to exercise the senses well about the right perceiving the differences of things, will be to lay the grounds for all wisdom, and all wise discourse, and all discreet actions in ones course of life. Which, because it is commonly neglected in schools, and the things which are to be learned are offered to scholars, without being understood or being rightly presented to the senses, it cometh to pass, that the work of teaching and learning goeth heavily onward, and affordeth little benefit.

See here then a new help for schools, A Picture and Nomenclature of all the chief things in the world, and of men's actions in their way of living: Which, that you, good Masters, may not be loath to run over with your scholars, I will tell you, in short, what good you may expect from it.

It is *a little Book*, as you see, of no great bulk, yet a brief of the whole world, and a whole language: full of Pictures, Nomenclatures, and Descriptions of things.

I. *The Pictures* are the representation of all visible things, (to which also things invisible are reduced after their fashion) of the whole world. And that in that very order of things, in which they are described in the *Janua Latinæ Linguæ;* and with that fulness, that nothing very necessary or of great concernment is omitted.

II. *The Nomenclatures* are the Inscriptions, or Titles set every one over their own Pictures, expressing the whole thing by its own general term.

III. *The Descriptions* are the explications of the parts of the Picture, so expressed by their own proper terms, as that same figure which is added to every piece of the picture, and the term of it, always sheweth what things belongeth one to another.

Which such Book, and in such a dress may (I hope) serve,

I. To entice witty children to it, that they may not conceit a torment to be in the school, but dainty fare. For it is apparent, that children (even from their infancy almost) are delighted with Pictures, and willingly please their eyes with these lights: And it will be very well worth the pains to have once brought it to pass, that scare-crows may be taken away out of Wisdom's Gardens.

II. This same little Book will serve to stir up the Attention, which is to be fastened upon things, and even to be sharpened more and more: which is also a great matter. For the Senses (being the main guides of childhood, because therein the mind doth not as yet raise up itself to an abstracted contemplation of things) evermore seek their own objects, and if they be away, they grow dull, and wry themselves hither and thither out of a weariness of themselves: but when their objects are present, they grow merry, wax lively, and willingly suffer themselves to be fastened upon them, till the thing be sufficiently discerned. This Book then will do a good piece of service in taking (especially flickering) wits, and preparing them for deeper studies.

III. Whence a third good will follow; that children being won hereunto, and drawn over with this way of heeding, may be furnished with the knowledge of the prime things that are in the world, by sport and merry pastime. In a word, this Book will serve for the more pleasing using of the *Vestibulum* and *Janua Linguarum*, for which end it was even at the first chiefly intended. Yet if it like any, that it be bound up in their native tongues also, it promiseth three good thing of itself.

I. First it will afford a device for learning to read more easily than hitherto, especially having a symbolical alphabet set before it, to wit, the characters of the several letters, with the image of that creature, whose voice that letter goeth about to imitate, pictur'd by it. For the young *Abc* scholar will easily remember the force of every character by the very looking upon the creature, till the imagination being strengthened by use, can readily afford all things; and then having looked over *a table of the chief syllables* also (which yet was not thought necessary to be added to this book) he may proceed to the viewing of the Pictures, and the inscriptions set over 'em. Where again the very looking upon the thing pictured suggesting the name of the thing, will tell him how the title of the picture is to be read. And thus the whole book being gone over by the bare titles of the pictures, reading cannot but be learned; and indeed too, which thing is to be noted, without using any ordinary tedious spelling, that most troublesome torture of wits, which may wholly be avoided by this method. For the often reading over the Book, by those larger descriptions of things, and which are set after the Pictures, will be able perfectly to beget a habit of reading.

II. The same book being used in English, in English Schools, will serve for the perfect learning of the whole English tongue, and that from the bottom; because by the aforesaid descriptions of things, the words and phrases of the whole language are found set orderly in their own places. And a short English Grammar might be added at the end, clearly resolving the speech already understood into its parts; shewing the declining of the several words, and reducing those that are joined together under certain rules.

III. Thence a new benefit cometh, that that very English Translation may serve for the more ready and pleasant learning of the Latin tongue: as one may see in this Edition, the whole book being so translated, that every where one word answereth to the word over against it, and the book is in all things the same, only in two idioms, as a man clad in a double garment. And there might be also some observations and advertisements added in the end, touching those things only, wherein the use of the Latin tongue differeth from the English. For where there is no difference, there needeth no advertisement to be given. But, because the first *tasks of learners ought to be little and single*, we have filled this first book of training one up to see a thing of himself, with nothing but rudiments, that is, with the chief of things and words, or with the grounds of the whole world, and the whole language, and of all our understanding about things. If a more perfect description of things, and a fuller knowledge of a language, and a clearer light of the understanding be sought after (as they ought to be) they are to be found somewhere whither there will now be an easy passage by this our *little Encyclopædia* of things subject to the senses. Something remaineth to be said touching the more chearful use of this book.

I. Let it be given to children into their hands to delight themselves withal as they please, with the sight of the pictures, and making them as familiar to themselves as may be, and that even at home before they be put to school.

II. Then let them be examined ever and anon (especially now in the school) what this thing or that thing is, and is called, so that they may see nothing which they know not how to name, and that they can name nothing which they cannot shew.

III. And let the things named them be shewed, not only in the Picture, but also in themselves; for example, the parts of the body, clothes, books, the house, utensils, *&c.*

IV. Let them be suffered also to imitate the Pictures by hand, if they will, nay rather, let them be encouraged, that they may be willing: first, thus to quicken the attention also towards the things; and to observe the proportion of the parts one towards another; and lastly to practise the nimbleness of the hand, which is good for many things.

V. If anything here mentioned, cannot be presented to the eye, it will be to no purpose at all to offer them by themselves to the scholars; as colours, relishes, *&c.*, which cannot here be pictured out with ink. For which reason it were to be wished, that things rare and not easy to be met withal at home, might be kept ready in every great school, that they may be shewed also, as often as any words are to be made of them, to the scholars.

Thus at last this school would indeed become a school of things obvious to the senses, and an entrance to the school intellectual. But enough: Let us come to the thing it self.

The Translator, to all judicious and industrious School-Masters.

Gentlemen.

There are a few of you (I think) but have seen, and with great willingness made use of (or at least perused,) many of the Books of this of this well-deserving Author Mr. John Comenius, which for their profitableness to the speedy attainment of a language, have been translated in several countries, out of Latin into their own native tongue.

Now the general verdict (after trial made) that hath passed, touching those formerly extant, is this, that they are indeed of singular use, and very advantageous to those of more discretion, (especially to such as already have a smattering of Latin) to help their memories to retain what they have scatteringly gotten here and there, to furnish them with many words, which (perhaps) they had not formerly read, or so well observed; but to young children (whom we have chiefly to instruct) as those that are ignorant altogether of things and words, and prove rather a meer toil and burthen, than a delight and furtherance.

For to pack up many words in memory, of things not conceived in the mind, is to fill the head with empty imaginations, and to make the learner more to admire the multitude and variety (and thereby, to become discouraged,) than to care to treasure them up, in hopes to gain more knowledge of what they mean.

He hath therefore in some of his latter works seemed to move retrograde, and striven to come nearer the reach of tender wits: and in this present Book, he hath, according to my judgment, descended to the very bottom of what is to be taught, and proceeded (as nature it self doth) in an orderly way; first to exercise the senses well, by representing their objects to them, and then to fasten upon the intellect by impressing the first notions of things upon it, and linking them on to another by a rational discourse. Whereas indeed, we, generally missing this way, do teach children as we do parrots, to speak they know not what, nay which is worse, we, taking the way of teaching little ones by Grammar only at the first, do puzzle their imaginations with abstractive terms and secondary intentions, which till they be somewhat acquainted with things, and the words belonging to them, in the language which they learn, they cannot apprehend what they mean. And this I guess to be the reason, why many great persons do resolve sometimes not to put a child to school till he be at least eleven or twelve years of age, presuming that he having then taken notice of most things, will sooner get the knowledge of the words which are applyed to them in any language. But the gross misdemeanor of such children for the most part, have taught many parents to be hasty enough to send their own to school, if not that they may learn, yet (at least) that they might be kept out of harm's way; and yet if they do not profit for the time they have been at school, (no respect at all being had for their years) the Master shall be sure enough to bear the blame.

So that a School-master had need to bend his wits to come within the compass of a child's capacity of six or seven years of age (seeing we have now such commonly brought to our Grammar-schools to learn the Latin Tongue) and to make that they may learn with as much delight and willingness, as himself would teach with dexterity and ease. And at present I know no better help to forward his young scholars than this little Book, which was for this purpose contrived by the Author in the German and Latin Tongues.

What profitable use may be had thereof, respecting chiefly that his own country and language, he himself hath told you in his preface; but what use we may here make of it in our Grammar-schools, as it is now translated into English, I shall partly declare; leaving all other men, according to my wont, to their own discretion and liberty, to use or refuse it, as they please. So soon then as a child can read English perfectly, and is brought to us to school to learn Latin, I would have him together with his Accidence, to be provided of this Book, in which he may at least once a day (beside his Accidence) be thus exercised.

I. Let him look over the pictures with their general titles and inscriptions, till he be able to turn readily to any one of them, and to tell its name either in English or Latin. By this means he shall have the method of the Book in his head; and be easily furnished with the knowledge of most things; and instructed how to call them, when at any time he meeteth with them elsewhere, in their real forms.

II. Let him read the description at large: First in English, and afterward in Latin, till he can readily read, and distinctly pronounce the words in both Languages, ever minding how they are spelled. And withal, let him take notice of the figures inserted, and to what part of the picture they direct by their like till he be well able to find out every particular thing of himself, and to name it on a sudden, either in English or Latin. Thus he shall not only gain the most primitive words, but be understandingly grounded in Orthography, which is a thing too generally neglected by us; partly because our English schools think that children should learn it at the Latin, and our Latin schools suppose they have already learn'd it at the English; partly, because our common Grammar is too much defective in this part, and scholars so little exercised therein, that they pass from schools to the Universities and return from thence (some of them) more unable to write true English, than either Latin or Greek. Not to speak of our ordinary Tradesmen, many of whom write such false English, that none but themselves can interpret what they scribble in their bills and shop-books.

III. Then let him get the Titles and Descriptions by heart, which he will more easily do, by reason of these impressions which the viewing of the pictures hath already made in his memory. And now let him also learn, 1. To construe, or give the words one by one, as they answer one another in Latin and English. 2. To Parse, according to the rules, (which I presume by this time) he hath learn'd in the first part of his Accidence; where I would have him tell what part of Speech any word is, and then what accidents belong to it; but especially to decline the nouns and conjugate the verbs according to the Examples in his Rudiments; and this doing will enable him to know the end and use of his Accidence. As for the Rules of Genders of Nouns, and the Præterperfect-tenses and Supines of Verbs, and those of Concordance and Construction in the latter part of the Accidence, I would not have a child much troubled with them, till by the help of this Book he can perfectly practise so much of Etymology, as concerns the first part of his Accidence only. For that, and this book together, being thoroughly learn'd by at least thrice going them over, will much prepare children to go chearfully forward in their Grammar and School-Authors, especially, if whilst they are employed herein, they be taught also to write a fair and legible hand.

There is one thing to be given notice of, which I wish could have been remedied in this Translation; that the Book being writ in high-Dutch doth express many things in reference to that Country and Speech, which cannot without alteration of some Pictures as well as words be expressed in ours: for the Symbolical Alphabet is fitted for German children rather than for ours. And whereas the words of that Language go orderly one for one with the Latin, our English propriety of Speech will not admit the like. Therefore it will behove those Masters that intend to make use of this Book, to construe it verbatim to their young Scholars, who will quickly learn to do it of themselves, after they be once acquainted with the first words of Nouns, and Verbs, and their manner of variation.

Such a work as this, I observe to have been formerly much desired by some experienced Teachers, and I my self had some years since (whilst my own Child lived) begun the like, having found it most agreeable to the best witted Children, who are most taken up with Pictures from their Infancy, because by them the knowledge of things which they seem to represent (and whereof Children are as yet ignorant) are most easily conveyed to the Understanding. But for as much as the work is now done, though in some things not so completely as it were to be wished, I rejoyce in the use of it, and desist in my own under takings for the present. And because any good thing is the better, being the more communicated; I have herein imitated a Child who is forward to impart to others what himself has well liked. You then that have the care of little Children, do not much trouble their thoughts and clog their memories with bare Grammar Rudiments, which to them are harsh in getting, and fluid in retaining; because indeed to them they signifie nothing, but a mere swimming notion of a general term, which they know not what it meaneth, till they comprehend particulars; but by this or the like subsidiary, inform them, first with some knowledge of things and words wherewith to express them, and then their Rules of speaking will be better understood and more firmly kept in mind. Else how should a Child conceive what a Rule meaneth, when he neither knoweth what the Latin word importeth, nor what manner of thing it is which is signified to him in his own native Language, which is given him thereby to understand the Rule? For Rules consisting of generalities, are delivered (as I may say) at a third hand, presuming first the things, and then the words to be already apprehended touching which they are made. I might indeed enlarge upon this Subject, it being the very Basis of our Profession, to search into the way of Childrens taking hold by little and little of what we teach them, that so we may apply ourselves to their reach: But I leave the observation thereof to your own daily exercise, and experience got thereby.

And I pray God, the fountain and giver of all wisdom, that hath bestowed upon us this gift of Teaching, so to inspire and direct us by his Grace, that we may train up Children in his Fear and in the knowledge of his Son Jesus Christ our Lord; and then no doubt our teaching and their learning of other things subordinate to these, will by the assistance of his blessed Spirit make them able and willing to do him faithful Service both in Church and Commonwealth, as long as they live here, that so they may be eternally blessed with him hereafter. This, I beseech you, beg for me and mine, as I shall daily do for you and yours, at the throne of God's heavenly grace; and remain while I live

Ready to serve you, as I truly love and honour you, and labour willingly in the same Profession with you, CHARLES HOOLE.

From my School, in
Lothbury, London, Jan. 25, 1658.

N. B. Those Heads or Descriptions which concern things beyond the present apprehension of Children's wits, as, those of Geography, Astronomy, or the like, I would have omitted, till the rest be learned, and a Child be *better able to understand them.*

The Judgment of Mr. Hezekiah Woodward, *sometimes an* eminent Schoolmaster in LONDON, *touching a work of this Nature; in his* Gate to Science, *chap.* 2.

Certainly *the use of Images or Representations is great:* If we could make our words as legible to Children as Pictures are, their information therefrom would be quickned and surer. But so we cannot do, though we must do what we can. And if we had Books, wherein are the Pictures of all Creatures, Herbs, Beasts, Fish, Fowls, they would stand us in great stead. For Pictures are the most intelligible Books that Children can look upon. They come closest to Nature, nay, saith Scaliger, Art exceeds her.

An Advertisement Concerning this Edition.

AS there are some considerable Alterations in the present Edition of this Book from the former, it may be expected an Account should be given of the Reasons for them. 'Tis certain from the Author's Words, that when it was first published, which was in Latin and Hungary, or in Latin and High-Dutch; every where one word answer'd to another over-against it: This might have been observ'd in our English Translation, which wou'd have fully answer'd the design of COMENIUS, and have made the Book much more useful: But Mr. Hoole, (whether out of too much scrupulousness to disturb the Words in some places from the order they were in, or not sufficiently considering the Inconveniences of having the Latin and English so far asunder) has made them so much disagree, that a Boy has sometimes to seek 7 or 8 lines off for the corresponding Word; which is no small trouble to Young Learners who are at first equally unacquainted with all Words, in a Language they are strangers to, except it be such as have Figures of Reference, or are very like in sound; and thus may perhaps, innocently enough join an Adverb in one Tongue, to a Noun in the other; whence may appear the Necessity of the Translation's being exactly literal, and the two Languages fairly answering one another, Line for Line.

If it be objected, such a thing cou'd not be done (considering the difference of the Idioms) without transplacing Words here and there, and putting them into an order which may not perhaps be exactly classical; it ought to be observed, this is design'd for Boys chiefly, or those who are just entering upon the Latin Tongue, to whom every thing ought to be made as plain and familiar as possible, who are not, at their first beginning, to be taught the elegant placing of Latin, nor from such short Sentences as these, but from Discourses where the Periods have a fuller Close. Besides, this way has already taken (according to the Advice of very good Judges,) in some other School-Books of Mr. Hoole's translating, and found to succeed abundantly well.

Such Condescensions as these, to the capacities of young Learners are certainly very reasonable, and wou'd be most agreeable to the Intentions of the Ingenious and worthy Author, and his design to suit whatever he taught, to their manner of apprehending it. Whose Excellency in the art of Education made him so famous all over Europe, as to be solicited by several States and Princes to go and reform the Method of their Schools; and whose works carried that Esteem, that in his own Life-time some part of them were not only translated into 12 of the usual Languages of Europe, but also into the *Arabic*, *Turkish*, *Persian*, and *Mogolic* (the common Tongue of all that part of the *East-Indies*) and since his death, into the *Hebrew*, and some others. Nor did they want their due Encouragement here in *England*, some Years ago; 'till by an indiscreet use of them, and want of a thorow acquaintance with his Method, or unwillingness to part from their old road, they began to be almost quite left off: Yet it were heartily to be wish'd, some Persons of Judgment and Interest, whose Example might have an influence upon others, and bring them into Reputation again, wou'd revive the COMENIAN METHOD, which is no other, than to make our Scholars learn with Delight and chearfulness, and to convey a solid and useful Knowledge of Things, with that of Languages, in an easy, natural and familiar way. *Didactic Works* (as they are now collected into one volume) for a speedy attaining the Knowledge of Things and Words, join'd with the Discourses of Mr. Lock* and 2 or 3 more out of our own Nation, for forming the Mind and settling good Habits, may doubtless be look'd upon to contain the most reasonable, orderly, and completed System of the Art of Education, that can be met with.

Yet, alas! how few are there, who follow the way they have pointed out? tho' every one who seriously considers it, must be convinc'd of the Advantage; and the generality of Schools go on in the same old dull road, wherein a great part of Children's time is lost in a tiresome heaping up a Pack of dry and unprofitable, or pernicious Notions (for surely little

*Mr. Lock's Essay upon Education.
Dr. Tabor's Christain Schoolmaster.
Dr. Ob. Walker of Education.
Mr. Monro's Essay on Education.
—His just Measures of the pious Institutions of Youth, &c

better can be said of a great part of that Heathenish stuff they are tormented with; like the feeding them with hard Nuts, which when they have almost broke their teeth with cracking, they find either deaf or to contain but very rotten and unwholesome Kernels) whilst Things really perfected of the understanding, and useful in every state of Life, are left unregarded, to the Reproach of our Nation, where all other Arts are improved and flourish well, only this of Education of Youth is at a stand; as if that, the good or ill management of which is of the utmost consequence to all, were a thing not worth any Endeavors to improve it, or was already so perfect and well executed that it needed none, when many of the greatest Wisdom and Judgment in several Nations, have with a just indignation endeavor'd to expose it, and to establish a more easy and useful way in its room.

'Tis not easy to say little on so important a subject, but thus much may suffice for the present purpose. The Book has merit enough to recommend it self to those who know how to make a right use of it. It was reckon'd one of the Author's best performances; and besides the many Impressions and Translations it has had in parts beyond Sea, has been several times reprinted here. It was endeavor'd no needless Alterations shou'd be admitted in this Edition, and as little of any as cou'd consist with the design of making it plain and useful; to shun the offence it might give to some; and only the Roman and Italic Character alternately made use of, where transplacing of Words cou'd be avoided.

London, J. H.
July 13, 1727.

Orbis Sensualium Pictus,

A World of Things Obvious to the Senses drawn in Pictures.

Invitation. I. Invitatio.

The Master and the Boy.	*Magister & Puer.*
M. Come, Boy, learn to be wise.	M. Veni, Puer, disce sapere.
P. What doth this mean, *to be wise?*	P. Quid hoc est, *Sapere?*
M. To understand rightly,	M. Intelligere recte,

to do rightly, and to speak out rightly all that are necessary.

P. Who will teach me this?

M. I, by God's help.

P. How?

M. I will guide thee thorow all.

I will shew thee all.

I will name thee all.

P. See, here I am; lead me in the name of God.

M. Before all things, thou oughtest to learn the plain *sounds*, of which man's *speech* consisteth; which *living creatures* know how *to make*, and thy *Tongue* knoweth how *to imitate*, and thy *hand* can *picture out*.

Afterwards we will go into the *World*, and we will view all things.

Here thou hast a lively and Vocal Alphabet.

agere recte, et eloqui recte omnia necessaria.

P. Quis docebit me hoc?

M. Ego, cum DEO.

P. Quomodo?

M. Ducam te per omnia.

Ostendam tibi omnia.

Nominabo tibi omnia.

P. En, adsum; duc me in nomine DEI.

M. Ante omnia, debes discere simplices *Sonos* ex quibus *Sermo* humanus constat; quos *Animalia* sciunt *formare*, & tua *Lingua* scit *imitari*, & tua *Manus* potest *pingere*.

Postea ibimus *Mundum*, & spectabimus omnia.

Hic habes vivum et vocale Alphabetum.

Cornix cornicatur, à à The *Crow* crieth.	A a
Agnus balat, b è è è The *Lamb* blaiteth.	B b
 *Cicàda* stridet, cì cì The *Grasshopper* chirpeth.	C c
 *Upupa* dicit, du du The *Whooppoo* saith.	D d
Infans ejulat, è è è The *Infant* crieth.	E e
 *Ventus* flat, fi fi The *Wind* bloweth.	F f
 *Anser* gingrit, ga ga The *Goose* gagleth.	G g
Os halat, hà'h hà'h The *Mouth* breatheth out.	H h
Mus mintrit, ì ì ì The *Mouse* chirpeth.	I i
 *Anas* tetrinnit, kha, kha The *Duck* quaketh.	K k
 *Lupus* ululat, lu ulu The *Wolf* howleth.	L
[mum *Ursus* murmurat, mum- The *Bear* grumbleth.	M m

 *Felis* clamat, The *Cat* crieth.	nau nau	N n
 *Auriga* clamat, The *Carter* crieth.	ò ò ò	O o
 *Pullus* pipit, The *Chicken* peepeth.	pi pi	P p
 *Cúculus* cuculat, The *cuckow* singeth.	kuk ku	Q q
 *Canis* ringitur, The *dog* grinneth.	err	R r
 *Serpens* sibilat, The *Serpent* hisseth.	si	S s
 *Graculus* clamat, The *Jay* crieth.	tac tac	T t
 *Bubo* ululat, The *Owl* hooteth.	ù ù	U u
 *Lepus* vagit, The *Hare* squeaketh.	va	W w
 *Rana* coaxat, The *Frog* croaketh.	coax	X x
 *Asinus* rudit, The *Asse* brayeth.	y y y	Y y
 *Tabanus* dicit, The *Breeze* or *Horse-flie* saith.	ds ds	Z z

God II. Deus.

God is of himself from everlasting to everlasting.

A most perfect and a most blessed *Being*.

In his *Essence* Spiritual, and One.

In his *Personality*, Three.

In his *Will*, Holy, Just, Merciful and True.

In his *Power* very great.

In his *Goodness*, very good.

In his *Wisdom*, unmeasurable.

A *Light* inaccessible; and yet all iu all.

Every where, and no where.

Deus est ex seipso, ab æterno in æternum.

Perfectissimum & beatissimum *Ens*.

Essentiâ Spiritualis & unus.

Hypostasi Trinus.

Voluntate, Sanctus, Justus, Clemens, Verax.

Potentiâ maximus.

Bonitate Optimus.

Sapientiâ, immensus.

Lux inaccessa; & tamen omnia in omnibus.

Ubique & nullibi.

The chiefest *Good*, and the only and inexhausted Fountain of all good things.	Summum *Bonum*, et solus et inexhaustus Fons omnium Bonorum.
As the *Creator*, so the *Governour* and *Preserver* of all things, which we call the *World*.	Ut *Creator*, ita *Gubernator* et *Conservator* omnium rerum,quas vocamus *Mundum*.

The World. III. Mundus.

The *Heaven*, 1.	*Cœlum*, 1.
hath *Fire*, and *Stars*.	habet *Ignem* & *Stellas*.
The *Clouds*, 2.	*Nubes*, 2.
hang in the *Air*.	pendent in *Aere*.
Birds, 3.	*Aves*, 3.
fly under the Clouds.	volant sub nubibus.
Fishes, 4.	*Pisces*, 4.
swim in the *Water*.	natant in *Aqua*.
The *Earth* hath *Hills*, 5.	*Terra* habet *Montes*, 5.
Woods, 6. *Fields*, 7.	*Sylvas*, 6. *Campos*, 7.
Beasts, 8. and *Men*, 9.	*Animalia*, 8. *Homines*, 9.

Thus the greatest *Bodies* of the World, the four *Elements*, are full of their own Inhabitants.	Ita maxima *Corpora* Mundi, quatuor *Elementa*, sunt plena Habitatoribus suis.

The Heaven. IV. Cœlum.

The Heaven, 1. is wheeled about, and encompasseth the *Earth*, 2. standing in the middle.	*Cœlum*, 1. rotatur, & ambit *Terram*, 2. stantem in medio.
The *Sun*, 3. wheresoever it is, shineth perpetually, howsoever dark *Clouds*, 4. may take it from us; and causeth by his *Rays*, 5. *Light*, and the Light, *Day*.	*Sol*, 3. ubi ubi est, fulget perpetuo, ut ut *densa* *Nubila*, 4. eripiant eum a nobis; facitque suis *Radiis*, 5. *Lucem*, Lux *Diem*.
On the other side, over against it, is *Darkness*, 6. and thence *Night*.	Ex opposito, sunt *Tenebræ*, 6. inde *Nox*.

In the Night shineth the *Moon*, 7. and the *Stars*, 8. glister and twinkle.	Nocte splendet *Luna*, 7. & *Stellæ*, 8. micant, scintillant.
In the Evening, 9. is *Twilight:*	Vesperi, 9. est *Crepusculum:*
In the *Morning*, 10. the breaking, and dawning of the Day.	Manè Aurora, 10. & Diluculum.

Fire. V. Ignis.

The *Fire* gloweth, burneth and consumeth to ashes.	*Ignis* ardet, urit, cremat.
A *spark* of it struck out of a *Flint* (or Firestone), 2. by means of a *Steel*, 1. and taken by *Tynder* in a *Tynder-box*, 3. lighteth a *Match*, 4. and after that a *Candle*, 5.	*Scintilla* ejus elisa e *Silice*, (Pyrite) 2. Ope *Chalybis*, 1. et excepta a *Fomite* in *Suscitabulo*, 3. accendit *Sulphuratum*, 4. et inde *Candelam*, 5.

or *stick*, 6.	vel *Lignum*, 6.
and causeth a *flame*, 7.	et excitat *Flammam*, 7.
or *blaze*, 8.	vel *Incendium*, 8.
which catcheth hold of	quod corripit
the Houses.	Ædificia.
Smoak, 9.	*Fumus*, 9.
ascendeth therefrom,	ascendit inde,
which, sticking to the	qui, adhærans
Chimney, 10.	*Camino*, 10.
turneth into *Soot*.	abit in *Fuliginem*.
Of a *Fire-brand*,	Ex *Torre*,
(or burning stick)	(ligno ardente,)
is made a *Brand*, 11.	fit *Titio*, 11.
(or quenched stick).	(lignum extinctum.)
Of a *hot Coal*	Ex *Pruna*,
(red hot piece	(candente particulâ
of a Fire-brand)	Torris.)
is made a *Coal*, 12.	fit *Carbo*, 12.
(or a *dead Cinder*).	(*Particula mortua*.)
That which remaineth,	Quod remanet,
is at last *Ashes*, 13.	tandem est *Cinis*, 13.
and *Embers* (or hot *Ashes*).	& *Favilla* (ardens *Cinis*.)

The Air. VI. Aër.

A cool *Air*, 1.	*Aura*, 1.
breatheth gently.	spirat leniter.
The *Wind*, 2.	*Ventus*, 2.
bloweth strongly.	flat valide.
A *Storm*, 3.	*Procella*, 3.
throweth down Trees.	sternit Arbores.
A *Whirl-wind*, 4.	*Turbo*, 4.
turneth it self in a round compass.	agit se in gyrum.
A Wind *under Ground*, 5.	Ventus *subterraneus*, 5.
causeth an *Earthquake*.	excitat *Terræ motum*.
An Earthquake causeth gapings of the Earth, (and falls of Houses.) 6.	Terræ motus facit Labes (& ruinas.) 6.

The Water. VII. Aqua.

The *Water* springeth	*Aqua* scatet
out of a *Fountain*, 1.	è *Fonte*, 1.
floweth downwards	defluit
in a *Brook*, 2.	in *Torrente*, 2.
runneth in a *Beck*, 3.	manat in *Rivo*, 3.
standeth in a *Pond*, 4.	stat in *Stagno*, 4.
glideth in a *Stream*, 5.	fluit in *Flumine*, 5.
is whirled about	gyratur
in a *Whirl-pit*, 6.	in *Vortice*, 6.
and causeth *Fens*, 7.	& facit *Paludes*, 7.
The *River* hath *Banks*, 8.	Flumen habet *Ripas*.
The *Sea* maketh *Shores*, 9.	*Mare* facit *Littora*, 9.
Bays, 10. *Capes*, 11.	*Sinus*, 10. *Promontoria*, 11.
Islands, 12. *Almost Islands*,	*Insulas*, 12. *Peninsulas*, 13.
13. *Necks of Land*, 14.	*Isthmos*, 14.
Straights, 15.	*Freta*, 15.
and hath in it *Rocks*, 16.	& habet *Scopulos*, 16.

The Clouds. VIII. Nubes.

A *Vapour*, 1. ascendeth from the *Water*.
From it a *Cloud*, 2. is made, and a *white Mist*, 3. near the Earth.
Rain, 4. and a small *Shower* distilleth out of a *Cloud*, drop by drop.
Which being frozen, is *Hail*, 5. half frozen is *Snow*, 6. being warm is *Mel-dew*.
In a rainy Cloud, set over against the Sun the *Rainbow*, 7. appeareth.
A *drop* falling into the water maketh a *Bubble*, 8. many *Bubbles* make froth, 9.
Frozen Water is called *Ice*, 10. *Dew* congealed,

Vapor, 1. ascendit ex *Aquâ*.
Inde *Nubes*, 2. fit, et *Nebula*, 3. prope terram.
Pluvia, 4. et *Imber*, stillat e *Nube*, guttatim.
Quæ gelata, *Grando*, 5. semigelata, *Nix*, 6. calefacta, *Rubigo* est.
In nube pluviosâ, opposità soli *Iris*, 7. apparet.
Gutta incidens in aquam, facit *Bullam*, 8. multæ *Bullæ* faciunt spumam, 9.
Aqua congelata *Glacies*, 10. *Ros* congelatus,

is called a *white Frost*.
Thunder is made of a brimstone-like *vapour*, which breaking out of a Cloud, with *Lightning*, 11. thundereth and striketh with lightning.

dicitur *Pruina*.
Tonitru fit ex *Vapore* sulphureo, quod erumpens è Nube cum *Fulgure*, 11. tonat & fulminat.

The Earth. IX. Terra.

In the *Earth* are
high *Mountains*, 1.
Deep *Vallies*, 2.
Hills rising, 3.
Hollow Caves, 4.
Plain *Fields*, 5.
Shady *Woods*, 6.

In *Terra* sunt
Alti *Montes*, 1.
Profundæ *valles*, 2.
Elevati Colles, 3.
cavæ Speluncæ, 4.
Plani *campi*, 5.
Opacæ Sylvæ, 6.

The Fruits of the Earth. X. Terræ Fœtus.

A *meadow*, 1. yieldeth *grass* with *Flowers* and *Herbs*, which being cut down, are made *Hay*, 2.	*Pratum*, 1. fert *Gramina*, cum *Floribus* & *Herbis* quæ defecta fiunt *Fœnum*, 2.
A *Field*, 3. yieldeth *Corn*, and *Pot-herbs*, 4.	*Arvum*, 3. fert *Fruges*, & *Olera*, 4.
Mushrooms, 5. *Straw-berries*, 6. *Myrtle-trees*, &c. *come up* in Woods.	*Fungi*, 5. *Fraga*, 6. *Myrtilli*, &c. *Proveniunt* in Sylvis.
Metals, *Stones*, and *Minerals* grow *under the earth*.	*Metalla*, *Lapides*, *Mineralia*, *nascuntur sub terra*.

Metals. XI. Metalla.

Lead, 1.
is soft, and heavy.
Iron, 2. is hard,
and *Steel*, 3. harder.
They make *Tankards*
(or *Cans*), 4. of *Tin*.
Kettles, 5. of *Copper*,
Candlesticks, 6. of *Latin*,
Dollers, 7. of *Silver*,
Ducats and *Crown-pieces*, 8.
Quick-silver is always liquid, and eateth thorow
Metals of Gold.

Plumbum, 1.
est molle & grave.
Ferrum, 2. est durum,
& *Calybs*, 3. durior.
Faciunt *Cantharos*, 4.
e *Stanno*.
Ahena, 5, e *Cupro*,
Candelabra, 6. ex *Orichalco*,
Thaleros, 7. ex *Argento*,
Scutatos et *Coronatos*, 8.
Ex, *Auro*.
Argentum Vivum, semper
liquet, & corrodit *Metalla*.

Stones. XII. Lapides.

Sand, 1. and *Gravel*, 2.
is *Stone* broken into bits.
A *great Stone*, 3.
is a piece of
a *Rock* (or Crag) 4.
A *Whetstone*, 5.
a *Flint*, 6. a *Marble*, 7. &c.
are ordinary Stones.
A *Load-stone*, 8.
draweth Iron to it.
Jewels, 9.
are clear Stones, as
The *Diamond* white,
The *Ruby* red,
The *Sapphire* blue,
The *Emerald* green,
The *Jacinth* yellow, &c.
And they glister
being cut into corners.
Pearls and *Unions*, 10.
grow in Shell-fish.

Arena, 1. & *Sabulum*, 2.
est *Lapis* comminutus.
Saxum, 3.
est pars
Petræ (Cautis) 4.
Cos, 5.
Silex, 6. *Marmor*, 7. &c.
sunt obscuri Lapides.
Magnes, 8.
adtrahit ferrum.
Gemmæ, 9.
sunt pellucidi Lapilli, ut
Adamas candidus,
Rubinus rubeus,
Sapphirus cæruleus,
Smaragdus viridis,
Hyacynthus luteus, &c.
et micant
angulati.
Margaritæ & *Uniones*, 10.
crescunt in Conchis.

Corals, 11. in a Sea-shrub.	*Corallia*, 11. in Marinâ arbusculâ.
Amber, 12. is gathered from the Sea.	*Succinum*, 12. colligitur è mari.
Glass, 13. is like *Chrystal.*	*Vitrum*, 13. simile est *Chrystallo.*

Tree. XIII. Arbor.

A *Plant*, 1. groweth from a *Seed.*	*Planta*, 1. procrescit e *Semine.*
A plant waxeth to a *Shoot*, 2.	Planta abit in *Fruticem*, 2.
A *Shoot* to a *Tree*, 3.	*Frutex* in *Arborem*, 3.
The *Root*, 4. beareth up the Tree.	*Radix*, 4. Sustentat arborem.
The *Body* or *Stem*, 5. riseth from the Root.	*Stirps* (*Stemma*) 5. Surgit e radice.
The *Stem* divideth it self into *Boughs*, 6. and green *Branches*, 7. made of *Leaves*, 8.	*Stirps* se dividit in *Ramos*, 6. & *Frondes*, 7. factas e *Foliis*, 8.

The *top*, 9.	*Cacumen*, 9.
is in the height.	est in summo.
The *Stock*, 10.	*Truncus*, 10.
is close to the roots.	adhærat radicibus.
A *Log*, 11.	*Caudex*, 11.
is the body fell'd down without Boughs; having *Bark* and *Rind*, 12. *Pith* and *Heart*, 13.	est Stipes dejectus, sine ramis; habens *Corticem* & *Librum*, 12. *pulpam* & *medullam*, 13.
Bird-lime, 14.	*Viscum*, 14.
groweth upon the boughs, which also sweat *Gumm*, *Rosin*, *Pitch*, &c.	adnascitur *ramis*, qui etiam sudant, *Gummi*, *Resinam*, *Picem*, &c.

Fruits of Trees. XIV. Fructus Arborum.

Fruits that have no shells are pull'd from fruit-bearing trees.	*Poma* decerpuntur, a fructiferis arboribus.
The *Apple*, 1. is round.	*Malum*, 1. est rotundum.

The *Pear*, 2. and *Fig*, 3.
are something long.
The *Cherry*, 4.
hangeth by a long start.
The *Plumb*, 5.
and *Peach*, 6.
by a shorter.
The *Mulberry*, 7.
by a very short one.
The *Wall-nut*, 8.
the *Hazel-nut*, 9.
and *Chest-nut*, 10.
are wrapped in a *husk*
and a *Shell*.
Barren trees are 11.
The *Firr*, the *Alder*,
The *Birch*, the *Cypress*,
The *Beech*, the *Ash*,
The *Sallow*, the *Linden-tree*,
&c., but most of them affording shade.
But the *Juniper*, 12.
and *Bay-tree*, 13. yield
Berries.
The *Pine*, 14. *Pine-apples*.
The *Oak*, 15.
Acorns and *Galls*.

Pyrum, 2. & *Ficus*, 3.
sunt oblonga.
Cerasum, 4.
pendet longo *Pediolo*.
Prunum, 5.
& *Persicum*, 6.
breviori.
Morum, 7.
brevissimo.
Nux Juglans, 8.
Avellana, 9.
& *Castanea*, 10.
involuta sunt *Cortici*
& *Putamini*.
Steriles arbores sunt 11.
Abies, *Alnus*,
Betula, *Cupressus*,
Fagus, *Fraxinus*,
Salix, *Tilia*, &c.
sed pleræque umbriferæ.
At *Juniperus*, 12.
& *Laurus*, 13. ferunt
Baccas.
Pinus, 14. *Strobilos*.
Quercus, 15.
Glandes & *Gallas*.

Flowers. XV. Flores.

Amongst the Flowers the most noted,	Inter flores notissimi,
In the beginning of the Spring are the *Violet*, 1. the *Crow-toes*, 2. the *Daffodil*, 3.	Primo vere, *Viola*, 1. *Hyacinthus*, 2. *Narcissus*, 3.
Then the *Lillies*, 4. white and yellow and blew, 5. and the *Rose*, 6. and the *Clove-gilliflowers*, 7. &c.	Tum *Lilia*, 4. alba & lutea, & cœrulea, 5. tandem *Rosa*, 6. & *Caryophillum*, 7. &c.
Of these *Garlands*, 8. and *Nosegays*, 9. are tyed round with twigs.	Ex his *Serta*, 8. & *Serviæ*, 9. vientur.
There are added also *sweet herbs*, 10. as *Marjoram*, *Flower gentle*, *Rue*, *Lavender*, *Rosemary*.	Adduntur etiam *Herbæ odoratæ*, 10. ut *Amaracus*, *Amaranthus*, *Ruta*, *Lavendula*, *Rosmarinus*, (Libanotis).

Hysop, *Spike*,
Basil, *Sage*,
Mints, &c.

Hypossus, *Nard*,
Ocymum, *Salvia*,
Menta, &c.

Amongst Field-flowers, 11. the most noted are the *May-lillie*, *Germander*, the *Blew-Bottle*, *Chamomel*, &c.

Inter Campestres Flores, 11. notissimi sunt *Lilium Convallium*, *Chamædrys*, *Cyanus*, *Chamæmelum*, &c.

And amongst Herbs, *Trefoil*. *Wormwood*, *Sorrel*, the *Nettle*, &c.

Et Herbæ, *Cytisus* (Trifolium) *Absinthium*, *Acetosa*, *Urtica*, &c.

The *Tulip*, 12. is the grace of flowers, but affording no smell.

Tulipa, 12. est decus Florum, sed expers odoris.

Potherbs. XVI. Olera.

Pot-herbs grow in Gardens, as *Lettice*, 1. *Colewort*, 2. *Onions*, 3.

Olera nascuntur in hortis, ut *Lactuca*, 1. *Brassica*, 2. *Cepa*, 3.

Garlick, 4. *Gourd*, 5.	*Allium*, 4. *Cucurbita*, 5.
The *Parsnep*, 6.	*Siser*, 6.
The *Turnep*, 7.	*Rapa*, 7.
The *Radish*, 8.	*Raphanus minor*, 8.
Horse-radish, 9.	*Raphanus major*, 9.
Parsly, 10.	*Petroselinum*, 10.
Cucumbers, 11.	*Cucumeres*, 11.
and *Pompions*, 12.	*Pepones*, 12.

Corn. XVII. Fruges.

Some *Corn* grows upon a *straw*, parted by *knots*, as *Wheat*, 1. *Rie*, 2, *Barley*, 3. in which the *Ear* hath *awnes*, or else it is without awnes, and it nourisheth the *Corn* in the *Husk*.	*Frumenta* quædam crescunt super *culmum*, distinctum *geniculis*, ut, *Triticum*, 1. *Siligo*, 2. *Hordeum*, 3. in quibus *Spica* habet *Aristas*, aut est mutica, fovetque *grana* in *gluma*.
Some instead of an ear, have a *rizom* (or plume) containing the corn by bunches, as *Oats*, 4. *Millet*, 5. *Turkey-wheat*, 6.	Quædam pro Spica, habent *Paniculam*, continentem grana fasciatim, ut, *Avena*, 4. *Milium*, 5. *Frumentum Saracenicum*, 6.

Pulse have *Cods*, which enclose the corns in two *Shales*, as *Pease*, 7. *Beans*, 8. *Vetches*, 9. and those that are less than these *Lentils* and *Urles* (or Tares).	*Legumina* habent *Siliquas*, quæ includunt grana *valvulis*, ut, *Pisum*, 7. *Fabæ*, 8. *Vicia*, 9. & minores his *Lentes* & *Cicera*.

Shrubs. XVIII. Frutices.

A plant being greater, and harder than an herb, is called a *Shrub*: such as are	Planta major & durior herba, dicitur *Frutex* : ut sunt
In Banks and Ponds, the *Rush*, 1. the *Bulrush*, 2. or Cane without knots bearing *Cats-tails*, and the *Reed*, 3. which is knotty and hollow within.	In ripis & stagnis, *Juncus*, 1. *Scirpus*, 2. [Canna] *enodis* ferens *Typhos*, & *Arundo*, 3. nodosa et cava intus.
Elsewhere, 4.	Alibi, 4.

the *Rose*,	*Rosa*,
the *Bastard-Corinths*,	*Ribes*,
the *Elder*, the *Juniper*.	*Sambucus*, *Juniperus*,
Also the *Vine*, 5. which	Item *Vitis*, 5.
putteth forth *branches*, 6.	quæ emittit *Palmites*, 6.
and these *tendrels*, 7.	et hi *Capreolos*, 7.
Vine-leaves, 8.	*Pampinos*, 8.
and Bunches of grapes, 9.	et *Racemos*, 9.
on the stock whereof	quorum Scapo
hang *Grapes*,	pendent *Uvæ*,
which contain *Grape-stones*.	continentes *Acinos*.

XIX.

Living-Creatures: and First, Birds.

Animalia: & primum, Aves.

A *living Creature* liveth,	*Animal* vivit,
perceiveth, moveth it self;	sentit, movet se;
is born, dieth,	nascitur, moritur,
is nourished,	nutritur,
and groweth: standeth,	& crescit; stat,
or sitteth, or lieth,	aut sedet, aut cubat,
or goeth.	aut graditur.

A *Bird*, (*Fisher*, 1. here the King's making her nest in the Sea.)	*Avis*, (hic *Halcyon*, 1. in mari nidulans.)
is covered with *Feathers*, 2.	tegitur *Plumis*, 2.
flyeth with *Wings*, 3.	volat *Pennis*, 3.
hath two *Pinions*, 4.	habet duas *Alas*, 4.
as many *Feet*, 5.	totidem *Pedes*, 5.
a *Tail*, 6.	*Caudam*, 6.
and a *Bill*, 7.	& *Rostrum*, 7.
The *Shee*, 8. *layeth* Eggs, 10. in a nest, 9.	*Fæmella*, 8. *ponit* Ova, 10. in nido, 9.
and sitting upon them,	et incubans iis,
hatcheth *young ones*, 11.	excludit *Pullos*, 11.
An *Egg* is cover'd with a *Shell*, 12.	*Ovum* tegitur *testa*, 12.
under which is the *White*, 13.	sub qua est *Albumen*, 13.
in this the *Yolk*, 14.	in hoc *Vitellus*, 14.

Tame Fowls. XX. Aves Domesticæ.

The *Cock*, 1. (which croweth in the Morning.)	*Gallus*, 1. (qui cantat mane.)

hath a *Comb*, 2.	habet *Cristam*, 2.
and *Spurs*, 3.	& *Calcaria*, 3.
being gelded, he is called	castratus dicitur
a *Capon*, and is crammed	*Capo* & saginatur
in a *Coop*, 4.	in *Ornithotrophico*, 4.
A *Hen*, 5.	*Gallina*, 5.
scrapeth the *Dunghil*,	ruspatur *fimetum*,
and picketh up Corns:	& colligit grana:
as also the *Pigeons*, 6.	sicut & *Columbæ*, 6,
(which are brought up in	(quæ educantur in *Colum-*
a *Pigeon-house*, 7.)	*bario*, 7.)
and the *Turkey-cock*, 8.	& *Gallopavus*, 8.
with his *Turkey-hen*, 9.	cum sua *Meleagride*, 9.
The gay *Peacock*, 10.	Formosus *Pavo*, 10.
prideth in his Feathers.	superbit pennis.
The *Stork*, 11.	*Ciconia*, 11.
buildeth her nest	nidificat
on the top of the House,	in tecto.
The *Swallow*, 12.	*Hirundo*, 12.
the *Sparrow*, 13.	*Passer*, 13.
the *Mag-pie*, 14.	*Pica*, 14.
the *Jackdaw*, 15.	*Monedula*, 15.
and the *Bat*, 16.	& *Vespertilio*, 16.
(or Flettermouse)	(Mus alatus)
use to flie about Houses.	volitant circa Domus.

Singing-Birds. XXI. Oscines.

The *Nightingal*, 1. singeth the sweetlyest of all.	*Luscinia* (*Philomela*), 1. cantat suavissime omnium.
The *Lark*, 2. singeth as she flyeth in the Air.	*Alauda*, 2. cantillat volitans in aere;
The *Quail*, 3. sitting on the ground;	*Coturnix*, 3. sedens humi;
others on the boughs of trees, 4. as the *Canary-bird*,	Cæteræ, in ramis arborum, 4. ut *Luteola* peregrina.
the *Chaffinch*,	*Fringilla*,
the *Goldfinch*,	*Carduelis*,
the *Siskin*,	*Acanthis*,
the *Linnet*,	*Linaria*,
the little *Titmouse*,	parvus *Parus*,
the *Wood-wall*,	*Galgulus*,
the *Robin-red-breast*,	*Rubecula*,
the *Hedge-sparrow*, &c.	*Curruca*, &c.
The party colour'd *Parret*, 5. the *Black-bird*, 6.	Discolor *Psittacus*, 5. *Merula*, 6.
the *Stare*, 7.	*Sturnus*, 7.
with the *Mag-pie*	cum *Pica*,
and the *Jay*, learn	& *Monedula*, discunt

to frame men's words.
A great many are wont to be shut in *Cages*, 8.

humanas voces formare
Pleræque solent includi *Caveis*, 8.

XXII.

Birds that haunt the Fields and Woods.

Aves Campestres & Sylvestres.

The *Ostrich*, 1. is the greatest Bird.
The *Wren*, 2. is the least.
The *Owl*, 3. is the most despicable.
The *Whoopoo*, 4. is the most nasty, for it eateth dung.
The *Bird of Paradise*, 5. is very rare.
The *Pheasant*, 6. the *Bustard*, 7.

Struthio, 1. ales est maximus.
Regulus, 2. (Trochilus) minimus.
Noctua, 3. despicatissimus.
Upupa, 4. sordidssimus, vescitur enim stercoribus.
Manucodiata, 5. rarissimus.
Phasianus, 6. *Tarda* (Otis), 7.

the deaf wild *Peacock*, 8.	surdus, *Tetrao*, 8.
the *Moor-hen*, 9.	*Attagen*, 9.
the *Partrige*, 10.	*Perdix*, 10.
the *Woodcock*, 11.	*Gallinago* (Rusticola), 11.
and the *Thrush*, 12.	& *Turdus*, 12,
are counted Dainties.	habentur in deliciis.
Among the rest,	Inter reliquas,
the best are,	potissimæ sunt,
the watchful *Crane*, 13.	*Grus*, 13. pervigil.
the mournful *Turtle*, 14.	*Turtur*, 14. gemens.
the *Cuckow*, 15.	*Cuculus*, 15.
the *Stock-dove*,	*Palumbes*,
the *Speight*, the *Jay*,	*Picus*, *Garrulus*,
the *Crow*, &c., 16.	*Cornix*, &c., 16.

Ravenous Birds. XXIII. Aves Rapaces.

The *Eagle*, 1.	*Aquila*, 1.
the King of Birds	Rex Avium,
looketh upon the Sun,	intuetur Solem.
The *Vulture*, 2.	*Vultur*, 2.
and the *Raven*, 3.	& *Corvus*, 3.

feed upon *Carrion*.

The *Kite*, 4. pursueth Chickens.
The *Falcon*, 5.
the *Hobbie*, 6.
and the *Hawk*, 7.
catch at little Birds.
The *Gerfalcon*, 8. catcheth Pigeons and greater Birds.

pascuntur *morticinis*, [cadaveribus.]

Milvus, 4. insectatur pullos gallinaceos.
Falco, 5,
Nisus, 6.
& *Accipiter*, 7.
captant aviculas.
Astur, 8. captat columbas & aves majores.

Water-Fowl. XXIV. Aves Aquaticæ.

The white *Swan*, 1.
the *Goose*, 2.
and the *Duck*, 3.
swim up and down.
The *Cormorant*, 4,
diveth.
And to these the water-hen, and the *Pelican*, &c., 10.

Oler, 1. candidus,
Anser, 2.
& *Anas*, 3.
natant.
Mergus, 4.
se mergit.
Adde his Fulicam,
Pelecanum, &c., 10.

The *Osprey*, 5.
and the *Sea-mew*, 6.
flying downwards
use to catch Fish,
but the *Heron*, 7.
standing on the Banks.
The *Bittern*, 8. putteth
his Bill in the water, and
belloweth like an Ox.
The *Water-wagtail*, 9.
waggeth the tail.

Haliœetus, 5.
& *Gavia*, 6.
devolantes,
captant pisces,
sed *Ardea*, 7.
stans in ripis.
Butio, 8.
inferit rostrum aquæ,
& mugit ut bos.
Motacilla, 9.
motat caudam.

Flying Vermin. XXV. Insecta volantia.

The *Bee*, 1. maketh honey
which the *Drone*, 2. devour-
eth. The *Wasp*, 3.
and the *Hornet*, 4.
molest with a sting;
and the *Gad-Bee*
(or Breese), 5.
especially *Cattel*;

Apis, 1. facit mel
quod *Fucus*, 2. depascit
Vespa, 3.
& *Crabro*, 4.
infestant oculeo;
& *Oestrum*
(Asilus), 5.
imprimis *pecus*.

but the *Fly*, 6.	autem *Musca*, 6.
and the *Gnat*, 7. us.	& *Culex*, 7. nos.
The *Cricket*, 8. singeth.	*Gryllus*, 8. *cantillat.*
The *Butterfly*, 9. is a winged *Caterpillar.*	*Papillio*, 9. est alata *Eruca.*
The *Beetle*, 10. covereth her wings with *Cases.*	*Scarabæus*, 10. tegit alas *vaginis.*
The *Glow-worm*, 11. shineth by night.	*Cicindela* [Lampyris], 11. nitet noctu.

XXVI.

Four-Footed Beasts: and First those about the House.

Quadrupeda: & primum Domestica.

The *Dog*, 1. with the *Whelp*, 2. is keeper of the House.	*Canis*, 1. cum *Catello*, 2. est custos Domûs.
The *Cat*, 3.	*Felis* (Catus) 3.

riddeth the House	purgat domum
of *Mice*, 4.	à *Muribus*, 4.
which also a	quod etiam
Mouse-trap, 5. doth.	*Muscipula*, 5. facit.
A *Squirrel*, 6.	*Sciurus*, 6.
The *Ape*, 7.	*Simia*, 7.
and the *Monkey*, 8.	& *Cercopithecus*, 8.
are kept at home	habentur domi
for delight.	delectamento.
The *Dormouse*, 9. and	*Glis*, 9. &
other greater Mice, 10.	cæteri Mures majores, 10.
as, the *Weesel*, the *Marten*,	ut, *Mustela*, *Martes*,
and the *Ferret*,	*Viverra*,
trouble the House,	infestant domum.

Herd-Cattle. XXVII. Pecora.

The *Bull*, 1. the *Cow*, 2.	*Taurus*, 1. *Vacca*, 2.
and the *Calf*, 3.	& *Vitulus*, 3.
are covered with hair.	teguntur pilis.
The *Ram*, the *Weather*, 4.	*Aries*, *Vervex*, 4.
the *Ewe*, 5. and the *Lamb*, 6.	*Ovis*, 5. cum *Agno*, 6.
bear wool.	gestant lanam.

The *He-goat*, the *Gelt-goat*, 7.	*Hircus*, *Caper*, 7.
with the *She-goat*, 8.	cum *Capra*, 8.
and *Kid*, 9. have	& *Hœdo*, 9. habent.
shag-hair and *beards*.	*Villos* & *aruncos*.
The *Hog*, the *Sow*, 10.	*Porcus*, *Scrofa*, 10.
and the *Pigs*, 11.	cum *Porcellis*, 11.
have *bristles*,	habent *Setas*,
but not *horns*;	at non *Cornua* ;
but also *cloven feet*	sed etiam *Ungulas bisulcas*
as those others (have.)	ut illa.

Labouring-Beasts. XXVIII. Jumenta.

The *Ass*, 1.	*Asinus*, 1.
and the *Mule*, 2.	& *Mulus*, 2.
carry burthens.	gestant Onera.
The *Horse*, 3.	*Equus*, 3.
(which a *Mane*, 4. graceth) carryeth us.	(quam *Juba*, 4. ornat) gestat nos ipsos.
The *Camel*, 5.	*Camelus*, 5.
carryeth the Merchant	gestat Mercatorem
with his Ware.	cum mercibus suis.

The *Elephant*, 6.
draweth his meat to him
with his *Trunk*, 7.
He hath two *Teeth*, 8.
standing out,
and is able to carry
full thirty men.

Elephas, (Barrus) 6.
attrahit pabulum
Proboscide, 7.
Habet duos *dentes*, 8.
prominentes,
& potest portare
etiam triginta viros.

Wild-Cattle. XXIX. Feræ Pecudes.

The *Buff*, 1.
and the *Buffal*, 2.
are wild Bulls.
The *Elke*, 3.
being bigger than an
Horse (whose back is im-
penetrable) hath knaggy
horns as also the *Hart*, 4.
but the *Roe*, 5. and
the *Hind-calf*, almost none.
The *Stone-back*, 6.
huge great ones.
The *Wild-goat*, 7.
hath very little ones,
by which she hangeth
her self on a Rock.

Urus, 1.
& *Bubalus*, 2.
sunt feri Boves.
Alces, 3.
major equo
(cujus tergus est impene-
trabilis) habet ramosa cor-
nua; ut & *Cervus*, 4.
Sed *Caprea*, 5.
cum *Hinnulo*, ferè nulla.
Capricornus, 6.
prægrandia;
Rupicapra, 7.
minuta,
quibus suspendit
se ad rupem.

The *Unicorn*, 8.	*Monoceros*, 8.
hath but one,	habet unum,
but that a precious one.	sed pretiosum.
The *Boar*, 9. assail-	*Aper*, 9.
eth one with his tushes.	grassatur dentibus.
The *Hare*, 10. is fearful.	*Lepus*, 10. pavet.
The *Cony*, 11.	*Cuniculus*, 11.
diggeth the Earth.	perfodit *terram* ;
As also the *Mole*, 12.	Ut & *Talpa*, 12.
which maketh hillocks.	quæ facit grumos.

Wild-Beasts. XXX. Feræ Besitæ.

Wild Beasts	*Bestiæ*
have sharp paws, and	habent acutos ungues, &
teeth, and are flesh eaters.	dentes,suntque carnivoræ,.
As the *Lyon*, 1.	Ut *Leo*, 1.
the King of four-footed	Rex quadrupedum,
Beasts, having a mane;	jubatus ;
with the *Lioness*.	cum *Leænâ*.
The spotted *Panther*, 2.	Maculosus, *Pardo* (Pan-thera) 2.

The *Tyger*, 3.
the cruellest of all.
The Shaggy *Bear*, 4.
The ravenous *Wolf*, 5.
The quick sighted *Ounce*,
6. The tayled *fox*, 7.
the craftiest of all.
The *Hedge-hog*, 8.
is prickly.
The *Badger*, 9.
delighteth in holes.

Tygris, 3.
immanissima omnium.
Villosus *Ursus*, 4.
Rapax *Lupus*, 5.
Lynx, 6. visu pollens,
Caudata *Vulpes*, 7.
astutissima *omnium*.
Erinaceus, 8.
est aculeatus.
Melis, 9.
gaudet latebris.

XXXI.
Serpents and Creeping things.

Serpentes & Reptilia.

Snakes creep
by winding themselves;
The *Adder*, 1.
in the wood;
The *Water-snake*, 2.
in the water;
The *Viper*, 3.
amongst great stones.

Angues repunt
sinuando se;
Coluber, 1.
in Sylvâ;
Natrix, (hydra) 2.
in Aquâ;
Vipera, 3.
in saxis;

The *Asp*, 4. in the fields.	*Aspis*, 4, in campis.
The *Boa*, (or Mild-snake) 5. in Houses.	*Boa*, 5. in Domibus.
The *Slow-worm*, 6. is blind.	*Cæcilia*, 6. est cœca.
The *Lizzard*, 7. and the *Salamander*, 8. (that liveth long in fire) have feet.	*Lacerta*, 7. *Salamandra*, 8. (in igne vivax,) habent pedes.
The *Dragon*, 9. *a winged Serpent*, killeth with his Breath.	*Draco*, 9. *Serpens alatus*, necat halitu.
The *Basilisk*, 10. with his Eyes;	*Basiliscus*, 10. Oculis;
And the *Scorpion*, 11. with his poysonous tail.	*Scorpio*, 11. venenatâ caudâ.

Crawling-Vermin. XXXII. Insecta repentia.

Worms gnaw *things*.	*Vermes*, rodunt *res*.

The *Earth-worm*, 1.	*Lumbricus*, 1.
the Earth.	terram.
The *Caterpillar*, 2.	*Eruca*, 2.
the Plant.	plantam.
The *Grashopper*, 3.	*Cicada*, 3.
the Fruits.	Fruges.
The *Mite*, 4. the Corn.	*Circulio*, 4. Frumenta.
The *Timber-worm*, 5.	*Teredo*, (cossis) 5.
Wood.	Ligna.
The *Moth*, 6. a garment.	*Tinea*, 6. vestem.
The *Book-worm*, 7.	*Blatta*, 7.
a Book.	Librum.
Maggots, 8.	*Termites*, 8.
Flesh and Cheese.	carnem & caseum.
Hand-worms, the Hair.	*Acari*, Capillum.
The skipping *Flea*, 9.	Saltans *Pulex*, 9.
the *Lowse*, 10.	*Pediculus*, 10.
and the stinking	fœtans *Cimex*, 11.
Wall-louse, 11. bite us.	mordent nos.
The *Tike*, 12.	*Ricinus*, 12.
is a blood-sucker.	sanguisugus est.
The *Silk-worm*, 13.	*Bombyx*, 13.
maketh silk.	facit sericum.
The *Pismire*, 14.	*Formica*, 14.
is painful.	est laboriosa.
The *Spider*, 15.	*Aranea*, 15.
weaveth a Cobweb,	texit Araneum,
nets for flies.	retia muscis.
The *Snail*, 16. carri-	*Cochlea*, 16.
eth about her Snail-horn.	circumfert testam.

XXXIII.

Creatures that live as well by Water as by Land.

Amphibia.

Creatures that live by land and by water, are	Viventia in terrâ & aquâ, sunt
The *Crocodile*, 1. a cruel and preying Beast of the River *Nilus*;	*Crocodilus*, 1. immanis & prædatrix bestia *Nili* fluminis;
The *Castor* or *Beaver*, 2. having feet like a Goose, and a scaly tail to swim.	*Castor*, (Fiber) 2. habens pedes anserinos & squameam Caudam ad natandum.
The *Otter*, 3.	*Lutra*, 3.
The croaking *Frog*, 4. with the *Toad*.	& coaxans *Rana*, 4. cum *Bufone*.
The *Tortoise*, 5. covered above and beneath with shells, as with a target.	*Testudo*, 5. Operta & infra, testis, ceu scuto.

XXXIV.

River Fish and Pond Fish.

Pisces Fluviatiles & Lacustres.

A *Fish* hath *Fins*, 1.
with which it swimmeth,
and *Gills*, 2.
by which it taketh breath,
and *Prickles*
instead of bones: besides
the *Male* hath a *Milt*,
and the *Female* a *Row*.

Some have *Scales*.
as the *Carp*, 3.
and the *Luce* or *Pike*, 4.

Some are sleek
as the *Eel*, 5.
and the *Lamprey*, 6.

The *Sturgeon*, 7.
having a sharp snout,
groweth beyond the
length of a Man.

The *Sheath-fish*, 8.

Piscis habet *Pinnas*, 1.
quibus natat;
& *Branchias*, 2.
quibus respirat;
& *Spinas*
loco ossium: præterea,
Mas Lactes,
Fœmina Ova.

Quidam habent *Squamas*,
ut *Carpio*, 3.
Lucius, (Lupus) 4.

Alii sunt glabri,
ut, *Anguilla*, 5.
Mustela, 6.

Accipenser (Sturio), 7.
mucronatus, crescit
ultra longitudinem viri.

Silurus, 8.

having wide Cheeks,
is bigger than he:
But the greatest,
is the *Huson*, 9.
Minews, 10.
swimming by shoals,
are the least.
Others of this sort are
the *Perch*, the *Bley*,
the *Barbel*,
the *Esch*, the *Trout*,
the *Gudgeon*, and *Trench*, 11.
The *Crab-fish*, 12. is covered with a shell, and it hath *Claws*, and crawleth forwards and backwards.
The *Horse-leech*, 13.
sucketh blood.

bucculentus,
major illo est:
Sed maximus
Antaseus (Huso,) 9.
Apuæ, 10.
natantes gregatim,
sunt minutissimæ.
Alii hujus generis sunt
Perca, *Alburnus*,
Mullus, (Barbus)
Thymallus, *Trutta*,
Gobius, *Tinca*, 11.
Cancer, 12.
tegitur *crusta*,
habetque *chelas*, & graditur porro & retrò.
Hirudo, 13.
sugit sanguinem.

XXXV.

Sea-fish, and Shell-fish. — Marini pisces & Conchæ.

The *Whale*, 1. is the greatest of the Sea-fish.

Balæna, (Cetus) 1. maximus Piscium marinorum.

The *Dolphin*, 2.	*Delphinus*, 2.
the swiftest.	velocissimus.
The *Scate*, 3.	*Raia*, 3.
the most monstrous.	monstrossimus.
Others are the *Lamprel*,4	Alii sunt *Murænula*, 4.
the *Salmon*, or the *Lax*, 5.	*Salmo*, (Esox) 5.
There are also fish that flie, 6.	Danturetiam volatiles,6.
Add *Herrings*, 7.	Adde *Haleces*, 7.
which arebroughtpickled,	qui salsi,
and *Place*, 8. and *Cods*, 9.	& *Passeres*,8. cum *Asellis*,9.
which are brought dry;	qui adferuntur arefacti;
and the Sea monsters,	& monstra marina,
the *Seal*. 10.	*Phocam*, 10.
and the *Sea-horse*, &c.	*Hippopotamum*, &c.
Shell-fish,11. have Shells.	*Concha*, 11. habet testas,
The *Oyster*, 12.	*Ostrea*, 12.
affordeth sweet meat.	dat sapidam carnem.
The *Purple-fish*, 13	*Murex*, 13.
purple;	purpuram;
The others, Pearls, 14.	*Alii*, 14. Margaritas.

Man. XXXVI. Homo.

Adam, 1. the first Man,	*Adamus*, 1. primus Homo,

was made by God after his own Image the sixth day of the Creation, of a lump of Earth.

And *Eve*, 2. the first Woman, was made of the Rib of the Man.

These, being tempted by the *Devil* under the shape of a *Serpent*, 3. when they had eaten of the fruit of the *forbidden Tree*, 4. were condemned, 5. to misery and death, with all their posterity, and cast out of *Paradise*, 6.

formatus est a Deo ad Imaginem suam sextâ die Creationis, e Gleba Terræ.

Et *Eva*, 2. prima mulier, formata est e costâ viri.

Hi, seducti *abolo* sub specie *Serpentis*, 3. cum comederent de fructu *vetitæ arboris*, 4. damnati sunt, 5. ad miseriam & mortem, cum omni posteritate sua, & ejecti e *Paradiso* 6.

XXXVII.
The Seven Ages of Man.

Septem Ætates Hominis.

A *Man* is first an *Infant*, 1. | *Homo* est primum *Infans*, 1.

then a *Boy*, 2.
then a *Youth*, 3.
then a *Young-man*, 4.
then a *Man*, 5.
after that an *Elderly-man*, 6.
and at last, a *decrepid old man*, 7.

So also in the other *Sex*, there are, a *Girl*, 8.
A *Damosel*, 9. a *Maid*, 10.
A *Woman*, 11.
an *elderly Woman*, 12. and a *decrepid old Woman*, 13.

deinde *Puer*, 2.
tum *Adolescens*, 3.
inde *Juvenis*, 4.
posteà *Vir*, 5.
dehinc *Senex*, 6.
tandem *Silicernium*, 7.

Sic etiam in altero *Sexu*, sunt, *Pupa*, 8.
Puella, 9. *Virgo*, 10.
Mulier, 11.
Vetula, 12.
Anus decrepita, 13.

XXXVIII.

The Outward Parts of a Man.

Membra Hominis Externa.

The *Head*, 1. is above, the *Feet*, 20. below.

Caput, 1. est supra, infra *Pedes*, 20.

the fore part of the Neck	Anterior pars Colli
(which ends at	(quod desit
the *Arm-holes*, 2.)	in *Axillas*, 2.)
is the *Throat*, 3. the	est *Jugulum*, 3.
hinder part, the *Crag*, 4.	posterior *Cervix*, 4.
The *Breast*, 5, is before;	*Pectus*, 5. est ante;
the *back*, 6, behind;	*Dorsum*, 6. retro;
Women have in it	Fœminis sunt in illo
two *Dugs*, 7.	binæ *Mammæ*, 7.
with *Nipples*,	cum *Papillis*.
Under the Breast	Sub pectore
is the *Belly*, 9.	est *Venter*, 9.
in the middle of it	in ejus medio,
the *Navel*, 10.	*Umbelicus*, 10.
underneath the *Groyn*, 11.	subtus *Inguen*, 11.
and the *privities*.	& *pudenda*.
The *Shoulder-blades*, 12.	*Scapulæ*, 12.
are behind the back,	sunt a tergo,
on which the *Shoulders*	â quibus pendent *humeri*,
depend, 13.	13.
on these the *Arms*, 14.	ab his *Brachia*, 14.
with the *Elbow*, 15. and then	cum *Cubito*, 15. inde ad
on either side the *Hands*,	utrumque Latus, *Manus*,
the *right*, 8. and the *left*, 16.	*Dextera*, 8. & *Sinistra*, 16.
The *Loyns*	*Lumbi*, 17.
are next the Shoulders,	excipiunt Humeros,
with the *Hips*, 18.	cum *Coxis*, 18.
and in the *Breech*,	& *in Podice*, (culo)
the *Buttocks*, 19.	*Nates*, 19.
These make the *Foot;*	Absolvunt Pedem;
the *Thigh*, 21. then the *Leg*,	*Femur*, 21. tum *Crus*, 23.
23. (the *Knee*, being be-	(*Genu*, 22. intermedio.)
twixt them, 22.)	
in which is the *Calf*, 24.	in quo *Sura*, 24.
with the *Shin*, 25.	cum *Tilia*, 25.
then the *Ankles*, 26.	abhinc *Tali*, 26.
the *Heel*, 27.	*Calx*, (Calcaneum) 27.
and the *Sole*, 28.	& *Solum*, 28.
in the very end,	in extremo
the great *Toe*, 29.	*Hallux*, 29.
with four (other) *Toes*.	cum quatuor *Digitis*.

XXXIX.

The Head and the Hand. — Caput & Manus.

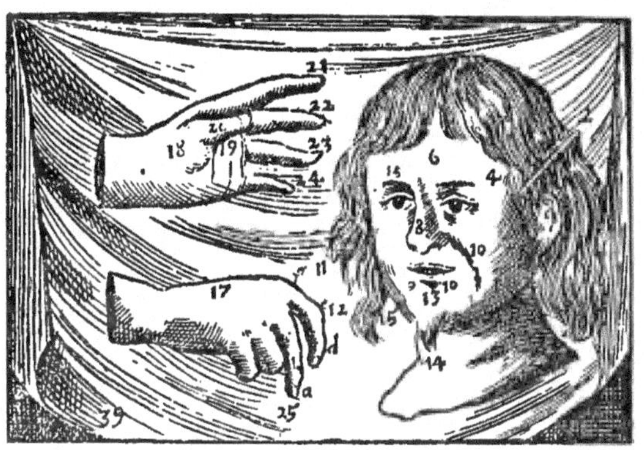

In the *Head* are
the *Hair*, 1.
(which is combed
with a *Comb*, 2.)
two *Ears*, 3.
the *Temples*, 4.
and the *Face*, 5.

In the Face are
the *Fore-head*, 6.
both the *Eyes*, 7.
the *Nose*, 8.
(with two *Nostrils*)
the *Mouth*, 9.
the *Cheeks*, 10.
and the *Chin*, 13.

The *Mouth* is fenced
with a *Mustacho*, 11.
and *Lips*, 12.

In *Capite* sunt
Capillus, 1.
(qui pectitur
Pectine, 2.)
Aures, 3. binæ,
& *Tempora*, 4.
Facies, 5.

In facie sunt
Frons, 6.
Oculus, 7. uterque,
Nasus, 8.
(cum duabus *Naribus*)
Os, 9.
Genæ, (Malæ) 10.
& *Mentum*, 13.

Os septum est
Mystace, 11.
& *Labiis*, 12.

A *Tongue* and a *Palate*,	*Lingua* cum *Palato*,
and *Teeth*, 16.	*Dentibus*, 16.
in the *Cheek-bone*.	in *Maxilla*.
A Man's Chin	Mentum virile
is covered with a *Beard*, 14.	tegitur *Barba*, 14.
and the Eye	Oculos vero
(in which is the *White*	(in quo *Albugo*
and the *Apple*)	& *Pupilla*)
with *eye-lids*,	*palpæbris*,
and an *eye-brow*, 15.	& *supercilio*, 15.
The *Hand* being closed	*Manus* contracta,
is a *Fist*, 17.	*Pugnus*, 17. est
being open is a *Palm*, 18.	aperta, *Palma*, 18.
in the midst, is the *hollow*, 19. of the Hand.	in medio *Vola*, 19.
the extremity is the *Thumb*, 20.	extremitas, *Pollex*, 20.
with four *Fingers*,	cum quatuor *Digitis*,
the *Fore-finger*, 21.	*Indice*, 21.
the *Middle-finger*, 22.	*Medio*, 22.
the *Ring-finger*, 23.	*Annulari*, 23.
and the *Little-finger*, 24.	& *Auriculari*, 24.
In every one are	In quolibet sunt
three *joynts*, a. b. c.	*articuli* tres, a. b. c.
and as many *knuckles*, d.e.f.	& totidem *Condyli*, d. e. f.
with a *Nail*, 25.	cum *Ungue*, 25.

The Flesh and Bowels. XL Caro & Viscera.

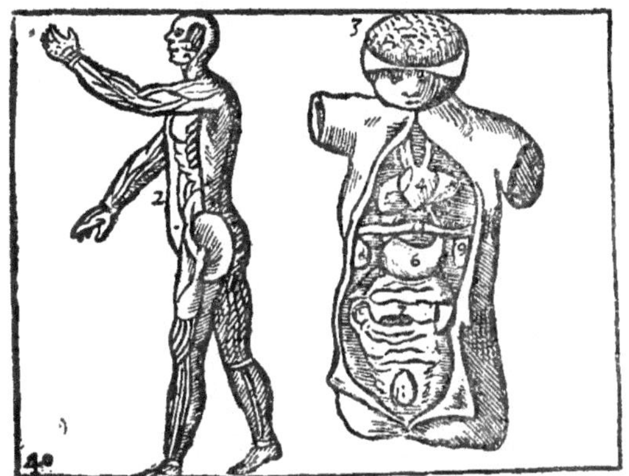

In the *Body* are the *Skin* with the *Membranes*, the *Flesh* with the *Muscles*, the *Chanels*, the *Gristles*, the *Bones* and the *Bowels*.

The *Skin*, 1. being pull'd off, the *Flesh*, 2. appeareth, not in a continual lump, but being distributed, as it were in stuft puddings, which they call *Muscles*, whereof there are reckoned four hundred and five, being the Chanels of the *Spirits*, to move the *Members*.

The *Bowels* are the inward *Members*:

As in the Head, the *Brains*, 3. being compassed about with a *Skull*, and

In *Corpore* sunt *Cutis* cum *Membranis*, *Caro* cum *Musculis*, *Canales*, *Cartilagines*, *Ossa* & *Viscera*.

Cute, 1. detractâ, *Caro*, 2. apparet, non continuâ massâ, sed distributa, tanquam in farcimina, quos vocant *Musculos*, quorum numerantur *quadringenti quinque*, canales *Spirituum*, ad movendum *Membra*.

Viscera sunt *Membra* interna:

Ut in Capite, *Cerebrum*, 3. circumdatum *Cranio*, &

the *Skin* which covereth the *Skull*.	*Pericranio*.
In the Breast, the *Heart*, 4. covered with a thin *Skin* about it, and the *Lungs*, 5. breathing to and fro.	In Pectore, *Cor*, 4. obvolutum *Pericardio*, & *Pulmo*, 5. respirans.
In the *Belly*,	In *Ventre*,
the *Stomach*, 6.	*Ventriculus*, 6.
and the *Guts*, 7.	& *Intestina*, 7.
covered with a *Caul*.	obducta *Omento*.
The *Liver*, 8.	*Jecur*, (Hepar) 8.
and in the left side opposite against it, the *Milt*, 9.	& à sinistro oppositus ei *Lien*, 9.
the two *Kidneys*, 10.	duo *Renes*, 10.
and the *Bladder*, 11.	cum *Vesica*, 11.
The Breast	Pectus
is divided from the Belly	dividitur à Ventre
by a thick Membrane,	crassâ Membranâ,
which is called	quæ vocatur
the *Mid-riff*, 12.	*Diaphragma*, 12.

The Chanels and Bones. XLI. Canales & Ossa.

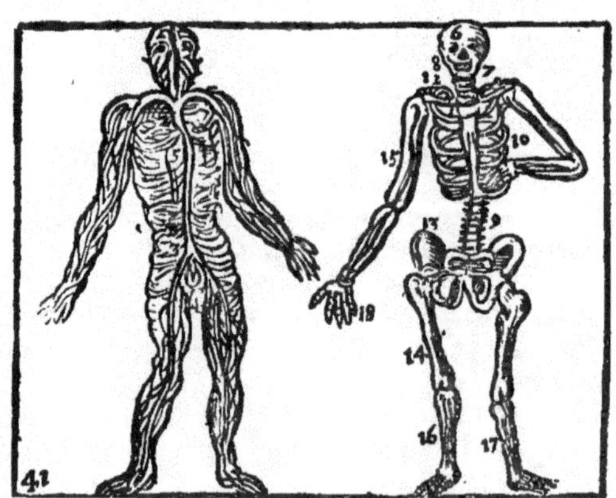

The Chanels of the Body are	Canales Corporis sunt

the *Veins*, carrying the Blood from the Liver;	*Venæ* deferentes Sanguinem ex Hepate;
The *Arteries* (carrying) *Heart* and *Life* from the *Heat*;	*Arteriæ*, *Calorem* & *Vitam* è *Corde*;
The *Nerves* (carrying) Sense and Motion throughout the Body from the *Brain*.	*Nervi*, Sensum et Motum, per Corpus a *Cerebro*.
You shall find these three, 1. everywhere joined together.	Invenies hæc tria, 1. ubique sociata.
Besides, from the Mouth into the Stomach is the *Gullet*, 2. the way of the meat and drink; and by it to the Lights, the *Wezand*, 5. for breathing; from the Stomach to the Anus is a great *Intestine*, 3. to purge out the *Ordure*; from the Liver to the Bladder, the *Ureter*, 4. for making water.	Porrò, ab Ore in Ventriculum *Gula*, 2. via cibi ac potus; & juxta hanc, ad Pulmonem *Guttur*, 5. pro respiratione; à ventriculo ad Anum *Colon*, 3. ad excernendum *Stercus*; ab Hepate ad Vesicam, *Ureter*, 4. reddendæ urinæ.
The *Bones* are in the Head, the *Skull*, 6. the two *Cheek-bones*, 7. with thirty-two *Teeth*, 8.	*Ossa* sunt in Capite, *Calvaria*, 6. duæ *Maxillæ*, 7. cum XXXII. *Dentibus*, 8.
Then the *Back-bone*, 9. the Pillar of the Body, consisting of thirty-four turning *Joints*, that the Body may bend it self.	Tum, *Spina dorsi*, 9. columna Corporis, constans ex XXXIV. *Vertebris*, ut Corpus queat flectere se
The *Ribs*, 10. whereof there are twenty-four.	*Costæ*, 10. quarum viginti quatuor.
The *Breast-bone*, 11. the two *Shoulder-blades*, 12. the *Buttock-bone*, 13. the *bigger Bone* in the Arm, 15. and the *lesser Bone* in the Arm.	*Os Pectoris*, 11. duæ *Scapulæ*, 12. *Os sessibuli*, 13. *Lacerti*, 15. & *Ulna*.

The *Thigh-bone*, 14.	*Tibia*, 14.
the foremost, 16.	*Fibula*, 16. anterior,
and the hindmost Bone,	& posterior, 17.
in the Leg, 17.	
The Bones of the Hand,	Ossa Manûs, 18.
18. are thirty-four, and	sunt triginta quatuor,
of the Foot, 19. thirty.	Pedis, 19. triginta.
The *Marrow* is in the	*Medulla* est in Ossibus,
Bones.	

XLII.
The Outward and Inward Senses.

Sensus externi & interni.

There are five outward	Sunt quinque externi
Senses;	*Sensus*;
The *Eye*, 1. seeth Col-	*Oculus*, 1. videt *Colores*,
ours, what is white or	quid album vel atrum,
black, green or blew,	viride vel cœruleum,
red or yellow.	rubrum aut luteum, sit.
The *Ear*, 2. heareth	*Auris*, 2. audit *Sonos*,
Sounds, both natural,	tum naturales,
Voices and Words;	Voces & Verba;
and artificial,	tum artificiales,

Musical Tunes.

The *Nose*, 3. scenteth smells and stinks.

The *Tongue*, 4. with the roof of the Mouth tastes *Savours*, what is sweet or bitter, keen or biting, sower or harsh.

The *Hand*, 5. by touching discerneth the quantity and quality of things; the hot and cold, the moist and dry, the hard and soft, the smooth and rough, the heavy and light.

The inward *Senses* are three.

The *Common Sense*, 7. under the *forepart of the head*, apprehendeth things taken from the outward Senses.

The *Phantasie*, 6. under the *crown of the head* judgeth of those things, thinketh and dreameth,

The *Memory*, 8. under the *hinder part of the head*, layeth up every thing and fetcheth them out: It loseth some, and this is *forgetfulness*.

Sleep, is the rest of the Senses.

Tonos Musicos.

Nasus, 3, *olfacit* odores & fœtores.

Lingua, 4. cum Palato gustat *Sapores*, quid dulce aut amarum, acre aut acidum, acerbum aut austerum.

Manus, 5. tangendo dignoscit quantitatem, & qualitatem rerum; calidum & frigidum, humidum & siccum, durum & molle, læve & asperum, grave & leve.

Sensus interni sunt tres.

Sensus Communis, 7. sub *sincipite* apprehendit res perceptas a Sensibus externis.

Phantasia, 6. sub *vertice*, dijudicat res istas, cogitat, somniat.

Memoria, 8. sub *occipitio*, recondit singula & depromit: deperdit quædam, & hoc est *oblivio*.

Somnus, est requies Sensuum.

The Soul of Man. XLIII. Anima hominis.

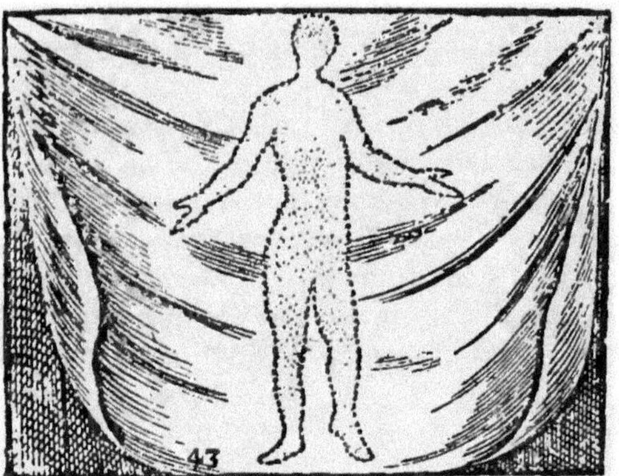

The *Soul* is the Life of the Body, one in the whole.

Only *Vegetative* in *Plants;*

Withal *Sensitive* in *Animals ;*

And also rational in *Men.*

This consisteth in three things;

In the *Understanding*,
whereby it judgeth
and understandeth
a thing good and evil,
or true, or apparent.

In the *Will*,
whereby it chooseth,
and desireth,
or rejecteth, and misliketh a thing known.

In the *Mind*,
whereby it pursueth

Anima est vita corporis, una in toto.

Tantùm *Vegetativa* in *Plantis* ;

Simul *Sensitiva* in *Animalibus ;*

Etiam *Rationalis* in *Homine.*

Hæc consistet in tribus:

In *Mente* (Intellectu)
quâ cognoscit,
& intelligit,
bonum ac malum,
vel verum, vel apparens.

In *Voluntate*,
quâ eligit,
& concupiscit,
aut rejicit,
& aversatur cognitum.

In *Animo*,
quo prosequitur

the Good chosen or avoideth the Evil rejected.
Hence is *Hope* and *Fear* in the desire, and dislike.
Hence is *Love* and *Joy*, in the Fruition:
But *Anger* and *Grief*, in suffering.
The true judgment of a thing is *Knowledge*; the false, is *Error*, *Opinion* and *Suspicion*.

Bonum electum, vel fugit Malum rejectum.
Hinc *Spes* & *Timor*, in cupidine, & aversatione:
Hinc *Amor* & *Gaudium*, in fruitione:
Sed *Ira* ac *Dolor*, in passione.
Vera cognitio rei, est *Scientia*; falsa, *Error*, *Opinio*, *Suspicio*.

XLIV.

Deformed and Monstrous People.

Deformes & Monstrosi.

Monstrous and *deformed* People are those which differ in the Body from the ordinary shape,

Monstrosi, & *deformes* sunt abeuntes corpore à communi formâ,

as the huge *Gyant*, 1.	ut sunt, immanis *Gigas*,
the little *Dwarf*, 2.	nanus (*Pumilio*), 2.
One with *two Bodies*, 3.	*Bicorpor*, 3.
One with *two Heads*, 4.	*Biceps*, 4.
and such like Monsters.	& id genus monstra.
Amongst these are reckoned, The *jolt-headed*, 5.	His accensentur, *Capito*, 5.
The great *nosed*, 6.	*Naso*, 6.
The *blubber-lipped*, 7.	*Labeo*, 7.
The *blub-cheeked*, 8.	*Bucco*, 8.
The *goggle-eyed*, 9.	*Strabo*, 9.
The *wry-necked*, 10.	*Obstipus*, 10.
The *great-throated*, 11.	*Strumosus*, 11.
The *Crump-backed*, 12.	*Gibbosus*, 12.
The *Crump-footed*, 13.	*Loripes*, 13.
The *steeple-crowned*, 15.	*Cilo*, 15.
add to these	adde
The *Bald-pated*, 14.	*Calvastrum*, 14.

XLV.

The Dressing of Gardens.	Hortorum cultura.

We have seen Man:	Vidimus hominem:
Now let us go on to Man's	Jam pergamus

living, and to *Handy-craft-Trades*, which tend to it.	ad *Victum* hominis, & ad *Artes Mechanicas*, quæ huc faciunt.
The first and most ancient *sustenance*, were the *Fruits of the Earth*.	Primus & antiquissimus *Victus*, erant *Fruges Terræ*.
Hereupon the first labour of Adam, was *the dressing of a garden*.	Hinc primus Labor Adami, *Horti cultura*.
The *Gardener*, 1.	*Hortulanus* (Olitor), 1.
diggeth in a *Garden-plot*,	fodit in *Viridario*,
with a *Spade*, 2.	*Ligone*, 2.
or *Mattock*, 3.	aut *Bipalio*, 3.
and maketh *Beds*, 4.	facitque *Pulvinos*, 4.
and places wherein to plant *Trees*, 5.	ac *Plantaria*, 5.
on which he setteth *Seeds* and *Plants*.	quibus inserit *Semina* & *Plantas*.
The *Tree-Gardener*, 6.	*Arborator*, 6.
planteth Trees, 7.	plantat Arbores, 7.
in an *Orchard*,	in *Pomario*,
and grafteth *Cyons*, 8.	*inseritque Surculos*, 8.
in *Stocks*, 9.	*Viviradicibus*, 9.
He fenceth his Garden,	Sepit hortum
either by care,	vel Cura,
with a *mound*, 10.	*Muro*, 10.
or a *Stone-wall*, 11.	aut *Macerie*, 11.
or a *rail*, 12.	aut *Vacerra*, 12.
or *Pales*, 13.	aut *Plancis*, 13.
or a *Hedge*, 14.	aut *Sepe*, 14.
made of *Hedge-stakes*,	flexâ è *sudibus*
and *bindings*;	& *vitilibus*;
Or by Nature, with *Brambles* and *Bryers*, 15.	Vel Natura *Dumis* & *Vepribus*, 15.
It is beautified with *Walks*, 16.	Ornatur *Ambulacris*, 16.
and *Galleries*, 17.	& *Pergulis*, 17.
It is watered with *Fountains*, 18.	Rigatur *Fontanis*, 18.
and a *Watering-pot*, 19.	& *Harpagio*, 19.

Husbandry. XLVI. Agricultura.

The *Plow-man*, 1.	*Arator*, 1.
yoketh *Oxen*, 3.	jungit *Boves*, 3.
to a *Plough*, 2.	*Aratro*, 2.
and holding the *Plow-stilt*,	& tenens *Stivam*, 4.
4. in his left hand,	lævâ,
and the *Plow-staff*, 5.	*Rallum*, 5.
in his right hand,	dextrâ,
with which he removeth	quâ amovet
Clods, 6.	*Glebas*, 6.
he cutteth the Land,	scindit terram
(which was manured afore	(stercoratam antea
with *Dung*, 8.)	*Fimo*, 8.)
with a *Share*, 7.	*Vomere*, 7.
and a *Coulter*,	et *Dentali*,
and maketh *furrows*, 9.	facitque *Sulcos*, 9.
Then he *soweth*	Tum *seminat*
the *Seed*, 10.	*Semen*, 10.
and harroweth it in	& inoccat
with a *Harrow*, 11.	*Occâ*, 11.
The *Reaper*, 12.	*Messor*, 12.
sheareth the ripe corn	metit fruges maturas
with a *Sickle*, 13. gather-	*Falce messoris*, 13.
eth up the *handfuls*, 14.	colligit *Manipulos*, 14.

and bindeth the *Sheaves*, 15.
The *Thrasher*, 16.
thrasheth Corn
on the *Barn-floor*, 17.
with a *Flayl*, 18. tosseth
it in a *winnowing-basket*, 19.
and so when the *Chaff*,
and the *Straw*, 20.
are separated from it, he
putteth it into *Sacks*, 12.
The *Mower*, 22.
maketh *Hay* in a *Meadow*,
cutting down *Grass*
with a *Sithe*, 23.
and raketh it together
with a *Rake*, 24. and
maketh up *Cocks*, 26.
with a *fork*, 25, and
carrieth it on *Carriages*, 27.
into the *Hay-barn*, 28.

& colligat *Mergetes*, 15.
Tritor, 16.
triturat frumentum
in *Area Horrei*, 17.
Flagello (tribula), 18.
jactat *ventilabro*, 19.
atque ita *Paleâ*
& *Stramine*, 20.
separatâ,
congerit in *Saccos*, 21.
Fœniseca, 22.
facit *Fœnum* in *Prato*,
desecans *Gramen*
Falce fœnaria, 23.
corraditque
Rastro, 24.
componit *Acervos*, 26.
Furca, 25. &
convehit *Vehibus*, 27.
in *Fœnile*, 28.

Grasing. XLVII. Pecuaria.

Tillage of ground,	*Cultus Agrorum,*
and *keeping Cattle,*	& *res pecuaria,*
was in old time the care	antiquissimis temporibus,
of Kings and Noble-men;	erat cura Regum, Heroum;
at this Day only of the	hodie tantum infirmæ
meanest sort of People.	Plebis,
The *Neat-heard*, 1.	*Bubulcus*, 1.
calleth out the *Heards*, 2.	evocat *Armenta*, 2.
out of the *Beast-houses*, 3.	è *Bovilibus*, 3.
with a *Horn*, 4.	*Buccina* (Cornu), 4,
and driveth them to feed.	& ducit pastum.
The *Shepherd*, 5.	*Opilio* (Pastor), 5.
feedeth his *Flock*, 6.	pascit *Gregem*, 6.
being furnished with a	instructus *Fistula*, 7.
Pipe, 7. and a *Scrip*, 8.	& *Pera*, 8.
and a *Sheep-hook*, 9.	ut & *Pedo*, 9.
having with him a great	habens secum *Molossum*,
Dog, 10.	10.
fenced with a *Collar*, 11.	munitum *Millo*, 11.
against the *Wolves*.	contra Lupos.
Swine, 12. are	*Sues*, 12. sagi-
fed out of a *Swine-Trough*.	nantur ex *aqualiculo haræ*.
The *Farmer's Wife*, 13.	*Villica*, 13.
milketh the *Udders*	mulget *Ubera*
of the *Cow*, 15.	*vaccæ*, 14.
at the *Cratch*, 15.	ad *Præsepe*, 15.
over a *milk-pale*, 16.	super *mulctra*, 16.
and maketh *Butter*	et facit *Butyrum*
of *Cream*	è *flore lactis*,
in a *Churn*, 17.	in *Vase butyraceo*, 17.
and *Cheeses*, 18.	et *Caseos*, 18.
of *Curds*.	è *Coagulo*.
The *Wool*, 19.	*Lana*, 19.
is shorn from *Sheep*,	detondetur *Ovibus*,
whereof several *Garments*	ex quà variæ *Vestes*
are made.	conficiuntur.

XLVIII.

The making of Honey. — Mellificium.

The *Bees* send out a *swarm*, 1. and set over it a *Leader*, 2.

That swarm being ready to fly away is recalled by the Tinkling of a *brazen Vessel*, 3. and is put up into a new *Hive*, 4.

They make little *Cells* with six corners, 5. and fill them with *Honey-dew*, and make *Combs*, 6. out of which the *Honey* runneth, 7.

The *Partitions* being melted by fire, turn into *Wax*, 8.

Apes emittunt *Examen*, 1. adduntque illi *Ducem* (Regem), 2.

Examen illud, avolaturum, revocatur tinnitu *Vasis æneì*, 3. & includitur novo *Alveari*, 4.

Struunt *Cellulas* sexangulares, 5. et complent eas *Melligine*, & faciunt *Favos*, 6. è quibus *Mel* effluit, 7.

Crates liquati igne abeunt in *Ceram*, 8.

Grinding. XLIX. Molitura

In a *Mill*, 1.	In *Mola*,
a Stone, 2. runneth	Lapis, 2. currit
upon a stone, 3.	super lapidem, 3,
A *Wheel*, 4.	*Rota*, 4.
turning them about	circumagente, et
and grindeth Corn poured	conterit grana infusa
in by a *Hopper*, 5.	per *Infundibulum*, 5.
and parteth the *Bran*, 6.	separatque *Furfurem*, 6.
falling into the *Trough*, 7.	decidentem in *Cistam*, 7.
from the *Meal* slipping	à *Farina* (Polline)
through a *Bolter*, 8.	elabente per *Excussorium*,8.
Such a Mill was first	Talis Mola primùm fuit
a *Hand-mill*, 9.	*Manuaria*, 9.
then a *Horse-mill*, 10.	deinde *Jumentaria*, 10.
then a *Water-mill*, 11.	tum *Aquatica*, 11.
then a *Ship-mill*, 12.	& *Navalis*, 12. tandem,
and at last a *Wind-mill*, 13.	*Alata* (pneumatica), 13.

Bread-baking. L. Panificium.

The *Baker*, 1.	*Pistor*, 1.
sifteth the *Meal*	cernit *Farinam*
in a *Rindge*, 2.	*Cribo*, 2. (pollinario)
and putteth it into the *Kneading-trough*, 3.	& indit *Mactræ*, 3.
Then he poureth water to it and maketh *Dough*, 4.	Tum affundit aquam, & facit *Massam*, 4.
and kneadeth it with a *wooden slice*, 5.	depsitque *spatha*, 5. ligneâ.
Then he maketh *Loaves*, 6. *Cakes*, 7. *Cimnels*, 8. *Rolls*, 9, &c.	Dein format *Panes*, 6. *Placentas*, 7. *Similas*, 8. *Spiras*, 9. &c.
Afterwards he setteth them on a *Peel*, 10.	Post imponit *Palæ*, 10.
and putteth them thorow the *Oven-mouth*, 12. into the *Oven*, 11.	& ingerit *Furno*, 11. per *Præfurnium*, 12.
But first he pulleth out the fire and the Coals with a *Coal-rake*, 13.	Sed priùs eruit ignem & Carbones *Rutabulo*, 13.

which he layeth on a heap underneath, 14.

And thus is *Bread* baked, having the *Crust* without, 15. and the *Crumb* within, 16.

quos congerit infra, 14.

Et sic *Panis* pinsitur habens extra *Crustam*, 15. intus *Micam*, 16.

Fishing. LI. Piscatio.

The *Fisher-man*, 1. catcheth fish, either on the Shoar, with an *Hook*, 2. which hangeth by a *Line* from the *angling-rod*, on which the *Bait* sticketh; or with a *Cleek-net*, 3. which hangeth on a *Pole*, 4. is put into the Water; or in a *Boat*, 5. with a *Trammel-net*, 6. or with a *Wheel*, 7. which is laid in the Water by Night.

Piscator, 1. captat pisces, sive in littore, *Hamo*, 2. qui pendet *filo* ab *arundine*, & cui *Esca* inhæret; sive *Fundâ*, 3. quæ pendens *Pertica*, 4. immittitur aquæ; sive in *Cymba*, 5. *Reti*, 6. sive *Nassa*, 7. quæ demergitur per Noctem.

Fowling. LII. Aucupium.

The *Fowler*, 1. maketh a *Bed*, 2, spreadeth a *Bird-net*, 3. throweth a *Bait*, 4. upon it, and hiding himself in a *Hut*, 5. he allureth Birds, by the chirping of *Lure-birds*, which partly hop upon the Bed, 6. and are partly shut in *Cages*, 7. and thus he entangleth Birds that fly over, in his net whilst they settle themselves down.

Auceps, 1. exstruit *Aream*, 2. superstruit illi *Rete* aucupatorium, 3. obsipat *Escam*, 4. & abdens se in *Latibulo*, 5. allicit Aves, cantu *Illicum*, qui partim in Area currunt, 6. partim inclusi sunt *Caveis*, 7. atque ita obruit transvolantes Aves Reti, dum se demittunt:

Or he setteth *Snares*, 8. on which they hang and strangle themselves:

Aut tendit *Tendiculas*, 8. quibus suspendunt & suffocant seipsas:

Or setteth *Lime-twigs*, 9. on a *Perch*, 10.

Aut exponit *Viscatos calamos*, 9. *Amiti*, 10.

upon which if they sit they enwrap their Feathers, so that they cannot fly away, and fall down to the ground.

quibus si insident, implicant pennas, ut nequeant avolare, & decidunt in terram.

Or he catcheth them with a *Pole*, 11. or a *Pit-fall*, 12.

Aut captat *Perticâ*, 11. vel *Decipulâ*, 12.

Hunting. LIII. Venatus.

The *Hunter*, 1. hunteth wild Beasts whilst he besetteth a Wood with *Toyls*, 2. stretched out upon *Shoars*, 3.

Venator, 1. venatur Feras, dum cingit Sylvam, *Cassibus*, 2. tentis super *Varos*, 3. (furcillas.)

The *Beagle*, 4. tracketh the wild Beast or findeth him out by the scent; the *Tumbler*, or *Greyhound*, 5. pursueth it.

Canis sagax, 4. vestigat Feram, aut indagat odoratu; *Vertagus*, 5. persequitur.

The *Wolf*, falleth in a *Pit*, 6.

Lupus, incidit in *Foveam*, 6.

the *Stag*, 7. as he runneth away, into *Toyls*.
The *Boar*, 8. is struck through with a *Hunting-spear*, 9.
The *Bear*, 10. is bitten by Dogs, and is knocked with a *Club*, 11.
If any thing get away, it escapeth, 12. as here a *Hare* and a *Fox*.

fugiens *Cervus*, 7. in *Plagas*.
Aper, 8. transverberatur *Venabulo*, 9.
Ursus, 10. mordetur à Canibus, & tunditur *Clavâ*, 11.
Si quid effugit, evadit, 12. ut hic *Lepus* & *Vulpes*.

Butchery. LIV. Lanionia.

The *Butcher*, 1. killeth *fat Cattle*, 2.
(The *Lean*, 3. are not fit to eat.)
He knocketh them down with an *Ax*, 4. or cutteth their Throat.

Lanio, 1. mactat *Pecudem altilem*, 2.
(*Vescula*, 3. non sunt vescenda.)
Prosternit *Clavâ*, 4. vel jugulat.

with a *Slaughter-knife*, 5.
he flayeth them, 6.
and cutteth them in pieces,
and hangeth out the flesh
to sell in the *Shambles*, 7.
He dresseth a *Swine*, 8.
with fire
or scalding water, 9.
and maketh *Gamons*, 10.
Pistils, 11.
and *Flitches*, 12.
Besides several *Puddings*,
Chitterlings, 13.
Bloodings, 14.
Liverings, 15.
Sausages, 16.
The *Fat*, 17. and
Tallow, 18. are melted.

Cunaculo, 5.
excoriat (deglubit,) 6.
dissecatque
& exponit carnes,
venum in *Macello*, 7.
Glabrat *Suem*, 8.
igne,
vel aquâ fervidâ, 9.
& facit *Pernas*, 10.
Petasones, 11.
& *Succidias*, 12.
Prætereà *Farcimina*
varia, *Faliscos*, 13.
Apexabones, 14.
Tomacula, 15.
Botulos, (Lucanicas) 16.
Adeps, 17. &
Sebum, 18. eliquantur.

Cookery. LV. Coquinaria.

The Yeoman of the Larder,
1. bringeth forth *Provision*,
2. out of the *Larder*, 3.

Promus Condus, 1.
profert *Obsonia*, 2.
è *Penu*, 3.

The *Cook*, 4. taketh them and maketh *several Meats*.

He first pulleth off the Feathers and draweth the Gutts out of the *Birds*, 5.

He scaleth and splitteth *Fish*, 6.

He draweth some flesh with *Lard*, by means of a *Larding-needle*, 7.

He caseth *Hares*, 8. then he boileth them in *Pots*, 9. and *Kettles*, 10. on the *Hearth*, 11. and scummeth them with a *Scummer*, 12.

He seasoneth things that are boyled with Spices, which he poundeth with a *Pestil*, 14. in a *Morter*, 13. or grateth with a *Grater*, 15.

He roasteth some on *Spits*, 16. and with a *Jack*, 17. or upon a *Grid-iron*, 18.

Or fryeth them in a *Frying-pan*, 19. upon a *Brand-iron*, 20.

Kitchen utensils besides are,
a *Coal-rake*, 21.
a *Chafing-dish*, 22.
a *Trey*, 23.
(in which *Dishes*, 24. and *Platters*, 25. are washed),
a pair of *Tongs*, 26.
a *Shredding-knife*, 27.
a *Colander*, 28.
a *Basket*, 29.
and a *Besom*, 30.

Coquus, 4. accipit ea & coquit *varia Esculenta*.

Prius deplumat, & exenterat *Aves*, 5.

Desquamat & exdorsuat *Pisces*, 6.

Trajectat quasdem carnes *Lardo*, ope *Creacentri*, 7.

Lepores, 8. exuit, tum elixat *Ollis*, 9. & *Cacabis*, 10. in *Foco*, 11. & despumat *Lingula*, 12.

Condit elixata, Aromatibus, quæ comminuit *Pistillo*, 14. in *Mortario*, 13. aut terit *Radulâ*, 15.

Quædam assat *Verubus*, 16. & *Automato*, 17. vel super *Craticulum*, 18.

Vel frigit *Sartagine*, 19. super *Tripodem*, 20.

Vasa Coquinaria præterea sunt,
Rutabulum, 21.
Foculus (Ignitabulum), 22.
Trua, 23.
(in quâ *Catini*, 24. & *Patinæ*, 25. eluuntur)
Forceps, 26.
Culter incisorius, 27.
Qualus, 28.
Corbis, 29.
& *Scopa*, 30.

The Vintage. LVI. Vindemia.

Wine groweth in the *Vine-yard*, 1. where *Vines* are propagated and tyed with Twigs to *Trees*, 2. or to *Props*, 3. or *Frames*, 4.

When the time of Grape-gathering is come, they cut off the *Bunches*, and carry them in *Measures of three Bushels*, 5. and throw them into a *Vat*, 6. and tread them with their *Feet*, 7. or stamp them with a *Wooden-Pestil*, 8. and squeeze out the juice in a *Wine-press*, 9. which is called *Must*, 11.

Vinum crescit in *Vinea*, 1. ubi *Vites* propagantur, & alligantur viminibus ad *Arbores*, 2. vel ad *Palos* (ridicas), 3. vel ad *Juga*, 4

Cùm tempus vindemiandi adest, abscindunt *Botros*, & comportant *Trimodiis*, 5. conjiciuntque in *Lacum*, 6. calcant *Pedibus*. 7. aut tundunt *Ligneo Pilo*, 8. & exprimunt succum *Torculari*, 9. qui dicitur *Mustum*, 11.

and being received in a great *Tub*, 10. it is poured into *Hogsheads*, 12. it is stopped up, 15. and being laid close in *Cellars* upon *Settles*, 14. it becometh *Wine*.

& exceptum *Orcâ*, 10. infunditur *Vasis* (Doliis), 12. operculatur, 15. & abditum in *Cellis*, super *Cantherios*, 14. abit in *Vinum*.

It is drawn out of the *Hogshead*, with a *Cock*, 13. or *Faucet*, 16. (in which is a *Spigot*) the Vessel being unbunged.

Promitur e *Dolio* *Siphone*, 13. aut *Tubulo*, 16. (in quo est *Epistomium*) Vase relito.

Brewing. LVII. Zythopoie.

Where *Wine* is not to be had they drink *Beer*, which is brewed of *Malt*, 1. and *Hops*, 2. in a *Caldron*, 3. afterwards it is poured into *Vats*, 4.

Ubi *Vinum* non habetur, bibitur *Cerevisia* (Zythus), quæ coquitur ex *Byne*, 1. & *Lupulo*, 2. in *Aheno*, 3. post effunditur in *Lacus*, 4.

and when it is cold,	& frigefactum.
it is carried in *Soes*, 5,	defertur *Labris*, 5.
into the *Cellar*, 6.	in *Cellaria*, 6.
and is put into Vessels.	& intunditur vasibus.
Brandy-wine, extracted by the power of heat from dregs of Wine in a *Pan*, 7. over which a *Limbeck*, 8. is placed, droppeth through a *Pipe*, 9. into a *Glass*.	*Vinum sublimatum*, extractum vi Caloris e fecibus Vini in *Aheno*, 7. cui *Alembicum*, 8. superimpositum est. destillat per *Tubum*, 9. in *Vitrum*.
Wine and Beer when they turn sowre, become *Vinegar*.	Vinum & Cerevisia, cum acescunt, fiunt *Acetum*.
Of Wine and Honey they make *Mead*.	Ex Vino & Melle faciunt *Mulsum*.

A Feast. LVIII. Convivium.

When a *Feast* is made ready,	Cum *Convivium* apparatur,
the table is covered with a *Carpet*, 1.	Mensa sternitur *Tapetibus*, 1.

and a *Table-cloth*, 2. by the *Waiters*, who besides lay the *Trenchers*, 3. *Spoons*, 4. *Knives*, 5. with little *Forks*, 6. *Table-napkins*, 7. *Bread*, 8. with a *Salt-seller*, 9.

Messes are brought in *Platters*, 10. a *Pie*, 19. on a *Plate*.

The Guests being brought in by the *Host*, 11. wash their Hands out of a *Laver*, 12. or *Ewer*, 14. over a *Hand-basin*, 13. or *Bowl*, 15. and wipe them on a *Hand-towel*, 16. then they sit at the Table on *Chairs*, 17.

The *Carver*, 18. breaketh up the good Cheer, and divideth it.

Sauces are set amongst *Roast-meat*, in Sawcers, 20.

The *Butler*, 21. filleth *strong Wine* out of a *Cruise*, 25. or *Wine-pot*, 26. or *Flagon*, 27. into *Cups*, 22. or *Glasses*, 23. which stand on a *Cupboard*, 24. and he reacheth them to the *Master of the Feast*, 28. who drinketh to his *Guests*.

& *Mappa*, 2. à *Tricliniariis*, qui præterea opponunt *Discos* (Orbes), 3. *Cochlearia*, 4. *Cultros*, 5. cum *Fuscinulis*, 6. *Mappulas*, 7. *Panem*, 8. cum *Salino*, 9.

Fercula inferuntur in *Patinis*, 10. *Artocrea*, 19. in *Lance*.

Convivæ introducti ab *Hospite*, 11. abluunt manus è *Gutturnio*, 12. vel *Aquali*, 14. super *Malluvium*, 13. aut *Pelvim*, 15. terguntque *Mantili*, 16. tum assident Mensæ per *Sedilia*, 17.

Structor, 18. deartuat dapes, & distribuit.

Embammata interponuntur *Assutaris* in Scutellis, 20.

Pincerna, 21. infundit *Temetum*, ex *Urceo*, 25. vel *Cantharo*, 26. vel *Lagena*, 27. in *Pocula*, 22. vel *Vitrea*, 23. quæ extant in *abaco*, 24. & porrigit, *Convivatori*, 28. qui propinat *Hospitibus*.

The Dressing of Line. LIX. Tractatio Lini.

Line and *Hemp*	*Linum* & *Cannabis*,
being rated in water,	macerata aquis,
and dryed again, 1.	et siccata rursum, 1.
are braked	contunduntur
with a *wooden Brake*, 2.	*Frangibulo ligneo*, 2.
where the *Shives*, 3. fall	ubi *Cortices*, 3. decidunt
down, then they are hec-	tum carminantur
kled with an *Iron Heckle*, 4.	*Carmine ferreo*, 4.
where the *Tow*, 5.	ubi *Stupa*, 5.
is parted from it.	separatur.
Flax is tyed to a *Distaff*,	*Linum purum* alligatur
6. by the *Spinster*, 7.	*Colo*, 6. à *Netrice*, 7.
which with her left hand	quæ sinistra
pulleth out the *Thread*, 8.	trahit *Filum*, 8.
and with her right hand	dexterâ, 12.
turneth a *Wheel*, 9.	*Rhombum* (girgillum), 9.
or a *Spindle*, 10. upon	vel *Fusum*, 10.
which is a *Wharl*, 11.	in quo *Verticillus*, 11.
The *Spool* receiveth	*Volva* accipit
the *Thread*, 13.	*Fila*, 13.

which is drawn thence	inde deducuntur
upon a *Yarn-windle*, 14.	in *Alabrum*, 14.
hence either *Clews*, 15.	hinc vel *Glomi*, 15.
are wound up,	glomerantur,
or *Hanks*, 16. are made.	vel *Fasciculi*, 16. fiunt.

Weaving. LX. Textura.

The *Webster*	*Textor*
undoeth the *Clews*, 1.	diducit *Glomos*, 1.
into *Warp*,	in *Stamen*,
and wrappeth it about	& circumvolvit
the *Beam*, 2.	*Jugo*, 2.
and as he sitteth	ac sedens
in his *Loom*, 3.	in *Textrino*, 3.
he treadeth upon the	calcat *Insilia*, 4.
Treddles, 4. with his Feet.	pedibus.
He divideth the *Warp*, 5.	Diducit *Stamen*, 5.
with *Yarn*.	*Liciis*,
and throweth the *Shuttle*, 6.	& trajicit *Radium*, 6.
through, in which is the	in quo est *Trama*,
Woofe, and striketh it close.	ac densat.

with the *Sley*, 7.	*Pectine*, 7.
and so maketh	atque ita conficit
Linen cloth, 8.	*Linteum*, 8.
So also the *Clothier*	Sic etiam *Pannifex*
maketh *Cloth* of *Wool.*	facit *Pannum* è *Lana.*

Linen Cloths. LXI. Lintea.

Linnen-webs	*Linteamina*
are bleached in the *Sun*, 1.	insolantur, 1.
with Water poured on	aquâ perfusâ, 2.
them, 2. till they be white.	donec candefiant.
Of them the *Sempster*, 3.	Ex iis *Sartrix*, 3.
soweth *Shirts*, 4.	suit *Indusia*, 4.
Handkirchers, 5.	*Muccinia*, 5.
Bands, 6. *Caps*, &c.	*Collaria*, 6. *Capitia*, &c.
These if they be fouled,	Hæc, si sordidentur
are washed again	lavantur rursum,
by the *Laundress*, 7. in	a *Lotrice*, 7. aquâ,
water, or *Lye* and *Sope.*	sive *Lixivio* ac *Sapone.*

The Taylor. LXII. Sartor.

The *Taylor*, 1. cutteth *Cloth*, 2. with *Shears*, 3. and seweth it together with a *Needle* and *double thread*, 4.

Then he presseth the *Seams* with a *Pressing-iron*, 5. And thus he maketh *Coats*, 6. with *Plaits*, 7. in which the *Border*, 8. is below with *Laces*, 9.

Cloaks, 10. with a *Cape*, 11. and *Sleeve Coats*, 12.

Doublets, 13. with *Buttons*, 14. and *Cuffs*, 15.

Breeches, 16. sometimes with *Ribbons*, 17.

Stockins, 18.

Gloves, 19.

Sartor, 1. discindit *Pannum*, 2. *Forfice*, 3. consuitque *Acu* & *Filo duplicato*, 4.

Posteâ complanat *Suturas Ferramento*, 5.

Sicque conficit *Tunicas*, 6. *Plicatas*, 7. in quibus infra est *Fimbria*, 8. cum *Institis*, 9.

Pallia, 10. cum *Patagio*, 11. & *Togas Manicatas*, 12.

Thoraces, 13. cum *Globulis*, 14. & *Manicis*, 15.

Caligas, 16. aliquando cum *Lemniscis*, 17.

Tibialia, 18.

Chirothecas, 19.

Muntero Caps, 20. &c.	*Amiculum*, 20. &c.
So the *Furrier*	Sic *Pellio*
maketh *Furred Garments*	facit *Pellicia*
of *Furs*.	è *Pellibus*.

The Shoemaker. LXIII. Sutor.

The *Shoemaker*, 1.	*Sutor*, 1.
maketh *Slippers*, 7.	conficit *Crepidas* (San-
Shoes, 8.	dalia,) 7. *Calceos*, 8.
(in which is seen	(in quibus spectatur
above, the *Upper-leather*,	superne *Obstragulum*,
beneath the *Sole*,	inferne *Solea*,
and on both sides	et utrinque
the *Latchets*)	*Ansæ*)
Boots, 9.	*Ocreas*, 9.
and *High Shoes*, 10.	et *Perones*, 10.
of *Leather*, 5.	e *Corio*, 5.
(which is cut with a	(quod discinditur
Cutting-knife), 6.	*Scalpro Sutorio*, 6.)
by means of an *Awl*, 2.	ope *Subulæ*, 2.
and *Lingel*, 3.	et Fili *picati*, 3.
upon a *Last*, 4.	super *Modum*, 4.

The Carpenter. LXIV. Faber lignarius.

We have seen Man's food and clothing: now his Dwelling followeth.	Hominis victum & amictum, vidimus: sequitur nunc Domicilium ejus.
At first they dwelt in *Caves*, 1. then in *Booths* or *Huts*, 2. and then again in *Tents*, 3. at the last in *Houses*.	Primò habitabant in *Specubus*, 1. deinde in *Tabernaculis* vel *Tuguriis*, 2. tum etiam in *Tentoriis*, 3. demum in *Domibus*.
The *Woodman* felleth and heweth down *Trees*, 5. with an *Ax*, 4. the *Boughs*, 6. remaining.	*Lignator* sternit & truncat *Arbores*, 5. *Securi*, 4. remanentibus *Sarmentis*, 6.
He cleaveth *Knotty Wood* with a *Wedge*, 7. which he forceth in with a *Beetle*, 8. and maketh *Wood-stacks*, 9.	Findit *Nodosum*, *Lignum Cuneo*, 7. quem adigit *Tudite*, 8. & componit *Strues*, 9.
The *Carpenter* squareth *Timber* with a *Chip-Ax*, 10.	*Faber Lignarius* ascit *Ascia*, 10. *Materiem*,

whence *Chips*, 11. fall, and saweth it with a *Saw*, 12. where the *Saw-dust*, 13. falleth down.

Afterwards he lifteth the *Beam* upon *Tressels*, 14. by the help of a *Pully*, 15. fasteneth it with *Cramp-irons*, 16. and marketh it out with a *Line*, 17.

Thus he frameth the *Walls* together, 18. and fasteneth the great pieces with *Pins*, 19.

unde *Assulæ*, 11. cadunt, & serrat *Serrâ*, 12. ubi *Scobs*, 13. decidit.

Post elevat *Tignum* super *Canterios*, 14. ope *Trochleæ*, 15. affigit *Ansis*, 16. & lineat *Amussi*, 17.

Tum compaginat *Parietes*, 18. & configit trabes *Clavis trabalibus*, 19.

The Mason. LXV. Faber Murarius,

The *Mason*, 1. layeth a *Foundation*, and buildeth *Walls*, 2.

Either of *Stones* which the *Stone-digger* getteth out of the *Quarry*, 3.

Faber Murarius, 1. ponit *Fundamentum*, & struit *Muros*, 2.

Sive è *Lapidibus*, quos *Lapidarius* eruit in *Lapicidina*, 3.

and the *Stone-cutter*, 4. squareth by a *Rule*, 5.

Or of *Bricks*, 6. which are made of *Sand* and *Clay* steeped in water, and are burned in fire.

Afterwards he plaistereth it with *Lime*, by means of a *Trowel*, and garnisheth with a *Rough-cast*, 8.

& *Latomus*, 4. conquadrat ad *Normam*, 5.

Sive è *Lateribus*, 6. qui formantur, ex *Arena* & *Luto*, aquâ intritis & excoquuntur igne.

Dein crustat *Calce*, ope *Trullæ*, 7. & vestit *Tectorio*, 8.

Engines. LXVI. Machinæ.

One can carry as much by thrusting a *Wheel-barrow*, 3. before him, (having an *Harness*, 4. hanging on his neck,) as two men can carry on a *Colestaff*, 1. or *Hand-barrow*, 2.

Unus potest ferre tantum trudendo *Pabonem*, 3. ante se, (*Ærumna*, Suspensâ a Collo) quantum duo possunt ferre *Palangâ*, vel *Feretro*, 2.

But he can do more that rolleth a Weight laid upon *Rollers*, 6. with a *Leaver*, 5.	Plus autem potest qui provolvit Molem impositam *Phalangis* (Cylindris, 6.) *Vecte*, 5.
A *Wind-beam*, 7. is a post, which is turned by going about it.	*Ergata*, 7. est columella, quæ versatur circumeundo.
A *Crane*, 8. hath a *Hollow-wheel*, in which one walking draweth weights out of a Ship, or letteth them down into a Ship.	*Geranium*, 8. habet *Tympanum*, cui inambulans quis extrahit pondera navi, aut demittit in navem.
A *Rammer*, 9. is used to fasten *Piles*, 10. it is lifted with a Rope drawn by *Pullies*, 11. or with hands, if it have *handles*, 12.	*Fistuca*, 9. adhibetur ad pangendum *Sublicas*, 10. adtollitur Fune tracto per *Trochleas*, 11. vel manibus, si habet *ansas*, 12.

A House. LXVII. Domus.

The *Porch*, 1. is before the *Door* of the *House*.	*Vestibulum*, 1. est ante *Januam* *Domûs*.

The *Door* hath
a *Threshold*, 2.
and a *Lintel*, 3.
and *Posts*, 4. on both sides.

The *Hinges*, 5.
are upon the right hand,
upon which the *Doors*, 6.
hang, the *Latch*, 7.
and the *Bolt*, 8.
are on the left hand.

Before the House
is a *Fore-court*, 9.
with a *Pavement*
of *square stones*, 10.
born up with *Pillars*, 11.
in which is the *Chapiter*, 12.
and the *Base*, 13.

They go up into the upper Stories by *Greess*, 14.
and *Winding-stairs*, 15.

The *Windows*, 16.
appear on the outside,
and the *Grates*, 17.
the *Galleries*, 18.
the *Watertables*, 19.
the *Butteresses*, 20.
to bear up the walls.

On the top is the *Roof*, 21.
covered with *Tyles*, 22.
or *Shingles*, 23.
which lie upon *Laths*, 24.
and these upon *Rafters*, 25.

The *Eaves*, 26.
adhere to the *Roof*.

The place without a Roof
is called an *open Gallery*, 27.

In the Roof are
Jettings out, 28.
and *Pinnacles*, 29.

Janua habet
Limen, 2.
& *Superliminare*, 3.
& *Postes*, 4. utrinque.

Cardines, 5.
sunt a dextris,
à quibus pendent *Fores*, 6.
Claustrum, 7.
aut *Pessulus*, 8.
a sinistris.

Sub ædibus
est *Cavædium*, 9.
Pavimento
Tessellato, 10.
fulcitum *Columnis*, 11.
in quibus *Peristylium*, 12.
& *Basis*, 13.

Ascenditur in superiores contignationes per *Scalas*, 14. & *Cocklidia*, 15.

Fenestræ, 16.
apparent extrinsecus,
& *Cancelli* (clathra), 17.
Pergulæ, 18.
Suggrundia, 19.
& *Fulcra*, 20.
fulciendis muris.

In summo est *Tectum*, 21.
contectum *Imbricibus* (*tegulis*), 22. vel *Scandulis*, 23.
quæ incumbunt *Tigillis*, 24. hæc *Tignis*, 25.

Tecto adhæret
Stillicidium, 26.

Locus sine Tecto
dicitur *Subdiale*, 27.

In Tecto sunt
Meniana, 28.
& *Coronides*, 29.

A Mine. LXVIII. Metallifodina.

Miners, 1.
go into the *Grave*, 2.
by a *Stick*, 3.
or by *Ladders*, 4.
with *Lanthorns*, 5.
and dig out with a
Pick, 6. the *Oar*,
which being put in *Baskets*,
7. is drawn out with a *Rope*,
8. by means of a *Turn*, 9.
and is carried
to the *Melting-house*, 10.
where it is forced with fire,
that the *Metal* may run
out, 12. the *Dross*, 11. is
thrown aside.

Metalli fossores, 1.
ingrediuntur *Puteum fodinæ*, 2. *Bacillo*, 3,
sive *Gradibus*, 4.
cum *Lucernis*, 5.
& effodiunt *Ligone*, 6.
terram Metallicam,
quæ imposita *Corbibus*, 7.
extrahitur *Fune*, 8.
ope *Machinæ tractoriæ*, 9.
& defertur
in *Ustrinam*, 10.
ubi urgetur igne,
ut *Metallum*, 12. profluat
Scoriæ, 11. abjiciuntur
scorsim.

The Blacksmith. LXIX. Faber Ferrarius.

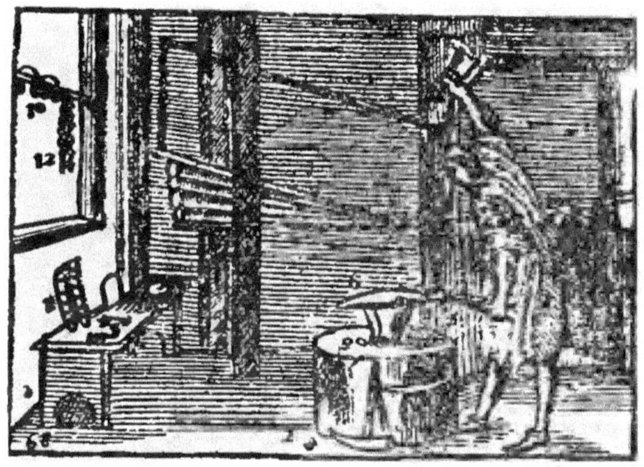

The *Blacksmith*, 1.
in his *Smithy* (or Forge), 2.
bloweth the fire
with a *pair of Bellows*, 3.
which he bloweth
with his *Feet*, 4.
and so heateth the *Iron*:
And then he taketh it
out with the *Tongs*, 5.
layeth it upon the *Anvile*, 6.
and striketh it
with an *Hammer*, 7.
where the *sparks*, 8. fly off.
And thus are hammer'd
out, *Nails*, 9.
Horse-shoes, 10.
Cart-strakes, 11.
Chains, 12.
Plates, *Locks* and *Keys*,
Hinges, &c.
He quencheth hot Irons
in a *Cool-trough*.

Faber ferrarius, 1.
in *Ustrina* (Fabricâ), 2.
inflat ignem
Folle, 3.
quem adtollit
Pede, 4.
atq; ita candefacit *Ferrum*:
Deinde eximit
Forcipe, 5.
imponit *Incudi*, 6.
& cudit
Malleo, 7.
ubi *Stricturæ*, 8. exiliunt.
Et sic excuduntur,
Clavi, 9.
Solea, 10.
Canthi. 11.
Catenæ, 12.
Laminæ, *Seræ* cum *Clavibus*,
Cardines, &c.
Restinguit cadentia,
Ferramenta in *Lacu*.

LXX.

The Box-maker and the Turner.

Scrinarius & Tornator.

The *Box-maker*, 1.	*Arcularius*, 1.
smootheth *hewen Boards*, 2.	edolat *Asseres*, 2.
with a *Plain*, 3.	*Runcina*, 3.
upon a *work-board*, 4. he	in *Tabula*, 4.
maketh them very smooth	deplanat
with a *little-plain*, 5.	*Planula*, 5.
he boreth them thorow	perforat (terebrat)
with an *Augre*, 6. carv-	*Terebra*, 6.
eth them with a *Knife*, 7.	sculpit *Cultro*, 7.
fasteneth them together	combinat
with *Glew* and *Cramp-Irons*,	*Glutine* & *Subscudibus*, 8.
8. and maketh *Tables*, 9.	& facit *Tabulas*, 9.
Boards, 10.	*Mensas*, 10.
Chests, 11. &c.	*Arcus* (Cistas), 11. &c.
The *Turner*, 12.	*Tornio*, 12.
sitting over the *Treddle*, 13.	sedens in *Insili*, 13.
turneth with a *Throw*, 15.	tornat *Torno*, 15.

upon a *Turner's Bench*, 14.	super *Scamno Tornatorio*,
Bowls, 16. *Tops*, 17,	14. *Globos*, 16. *Conos*, 17.
Puppets, 18. and	*Icunculas*, 18. &
such like *Turners Work*.	similia *Toreumata*.

The Potter. LXXI. Figulus.

The *Potter*, 1.	*Figulas*, 1.
sitting over a *Wheel*, 2.	sedens super *Rota*, 2.
maketh *Pots*, 4.	format *Ollas*, 4.
Pitchers, 5.	*Urceos*, 5.
Pipkins, 6.	*Tripodes*, 6.
Platters, 7.	*Patinas*, 7.
Pudding-pans, 8.	*Vasa testacea*, 8.
Juggs, 9.	*Fidelias*, 9.
Lids, 10. &c.	*Opercula*, 10. &c.
of *Potter's Clay*, 3.	ex *Argillâ*, 3.
afterwards he baketh them	postea excoquit
in an *Oven*, 11.	in *Furno*, 11.
and glazeth them	& incrustat
with *White Lead*.	*Lithargyro*.
A broken Pot affordeth	Fracta Olla dat
Pot-sheards, 12.	*Testas*, 12.

The Parts of a House. LXXII. Partes Domus

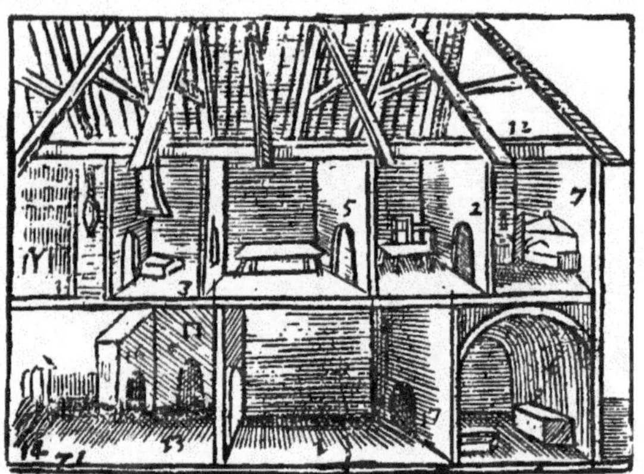

A *House* is divided into inner *Rooms*, such as are the *Entry*, 1. the *Stove*, 2. the *Kitchen*, 3. the *Buttery*, 4. the *Dining Room*, 5. the *Gallery*, 6. the *Bed Chamber*, 7. with a *Privy*, 8. made by it.

Domus distinguitur in *Conclavia*, ut sunt *Atrium*, 1. *Hypocaustum*, 2. *Cella Penuaria*, 4. *Cœnaculum*, 5. *Camera*, 6. *Cubiculum*, 7. cum *Secessu* (Latrina), 8. adstructo.

Baskets, 9. are of use for carrying things. and *Chests*, 10. (which are made fast with a *Key*, 11.) for keeping them.

Corbes, 9. inserviunt rebus transferendis, *Arcæ*, 10. (quæ *Clavâ*, 11. recluduntur) adfervandis illis.

Under the *Roof*, is the *Floor*, 12.

Sub *Tecto*, est *Solum* (Pavimentum), 12.

In the *Yard*, 13. is a *Well*, 14. a *Stable*, 15.

In *Area*, 13. *Puteus*, 14. *Stabulum*, 15.

and a *Bath*, 16.
Under the House
is the *Cellar*, 17.

cum *Balneo*, 16.
Sub Domo
est *Cella*, 17.

LXXIII.
The Stove with the Bed-room.

Hypocaustum cum Dormitorio.

The *Stove*, 1.
is beautified
with an *Arched Roof*, 2.
and *wainscoted Walls*, 3.
It is enlightened
with *Windows*, 4.
It is heated
with an *Oven*, 5.
Its Utensils are
Benches, 6.
Stools, 7.
Tables, 8.
with *Tressels*, 9.
Footstools, 10.
and *Cushions*, 11.

Hypocaustum, 1.
ornatur
Laqueari, 2.
& *tabulatis Parietibus*, 3.
Illuminatur
Fenestris, 4.
Calefit
Fornace, 5.
Ejus Utensilia sunt
Scamna, 6.
Sellæ, 7.
Mensæ, 8.
cum *Fulcris*, 9.
ac *Scabellis*, 10.
& *Culcitris*, 11.

There are also *Tapestries* hanged, 12.	Appenduntur etiam *Tapetes*, 12.
For soft lodging in a *Sleeping-room*, 13. there is a *Bed*, 14. spread on a *Bed-sted*, 15. upon a *Straw-pad*, 16. with *Sheets*, 17. and *Cover-lids*, 18.	Pro levi cubatu, in *Dormitorio*, 13. est *Lectus*, (Cubile) 14. stratus in *Sponda*, 15. super *Stramentum*, 16. cum *Lodicibus*, 17. & *Stragulis*, 18.
The *Bolster*, 19. is under ones head.	*Cervical*, 19. est sub capite.
The Bed is covered with a *Canopy*, 20.	*Canopeo*, 20. *Lectus* tegitur.
A *Chamber-pot*, 21. is for making water in.	*Matula*, 21. est vesicæ levandæ.

Wells. LXXIV. Putei.

Where *Springs* are wanting, *Wells*, 1. are digged. and they are compassed about with a *Brandrith*, 2. lest any one fall in.	Ubi *Fontes* deficiunt, *Putei*, 1. effodiuntur, & circumdantur *Crepidine*, 2. ne quis incidat.
Thence is water drawn	Inde aqua hauritur

with *Buckets*, 3.	*Urnis* (situlis), 3.
hanging either at a *Pole*, 4.	pendentibus vel *Pertica*, 4.
or a *Rope*, 5.	vel *Fune*, 5.
or a *Chain*, 6.	vel *Catena*, 6.
and that either by a *Swipe*,	idque aut *Tollenone*, 7.
7. or a *Windle*, 8.	aut *Girgillo*, 8.
or a *Turn*, 9.	aut *Cylindro*, 9.
with a *Handle*	*Manubriato*.
or a *Wheel*, 10.	aut *Rota* (tympano), 10.
or to conclude,	aut deinque
by a *Pump*, 11.	*Antliâ*, 11.

The Bath. LXXV. Balneum.

He that desireth to be	Qui cupit lavari
wash'd in cold water,	aquâ frigidâ,
goeth down into a *River*, 1.	descendit in *Fluvium*, 1.
In a *Bathing-house*, 2.	In *Balneario*, 2.
we wash off the *filth*	abluimus *squalores*,
either sitting in a *Tub*, 3.	sive sedentes in *Labro*, 3.
or going up	sive conscendentes
into the *Hot-house*, 4.	in *Sudatorium*, 4.

and we are rubbed	& defricamur
with a *Pumice-stone*, 6.	*Pumice*, 6.
or a *Hair-cloth*, 5.	aut *Cilicio*, 5.
In the *Stripping-room*, 7.	In *Apodyterio*, 7.
we put off our clothes,	exuimus Vestes,
and are tyed about	& præcingimur *Castula*
with an *Apron*, 8.	(Subligari), 8.
We cover our Head	Tegimus caput
with a *Cap*, 9.	*Pileolo*, 9.
and put our feet	& imponimus pedes
into a *Bason*, 10.	*Telluvio*, 10.
The *Bath-woman*, 11.	*Balneatrix*, 11.
reacheth water in a *Bucket*,	ministrat aquam *Situla*, 12.
12. drawn out of the	haustam ex *Alveo*, 13.
Trough, 13. into which it	in quem defluit
runneth out of *Pipes*, 14.	è *Canalibus*, 14.
The *Bath-keeper*, 15.	*Balneator*, 15.
lanceth with a *Lancet*, 16.	scarificat *Scalpro*, 16.
and by applying	& applicando
Cupping-glasses, 17.	*Cucurbitas*, 17.
he draweth the *Blood*	extrahit *Sanguinem*
betwixt the skin and the	subcutaneum,
flesh, which he wipeth	quem abstergit
away with a *Spunge*, 18.	*Spongiâ*, 18.

The Barbers Shop. LXXVI. Tonstrina.

The *Barber*, 1.	*Tonsor*, 1.
in the *Barbers-shop*, 2.	in' *Tonstrina*, 2.
cutteth off the *Hair*	tondet *Crines*
and the *Beard*	& *Barbam*
with a pair of *Sizzars*, 3.	*Forcipe*, 3.
or shaveth with a *Razor*,	vel radit *Novaculâ*,
which he taketh	quam depromit
out of his *Case*, 4.	è *Theca*, 4.
And he washeth one	Et lavat
over a *Bason*, 5.	super *Pelvim*, 5.
with *Suds* running	*Lixivio* defluente
out of a *Laver*, 6.	è *Gulturnio*, 6.
and also with *Sope*, 7.	ut & *Sapone*, 7.
and wipeth him	& tergit
with a *Towel*, 8.	*Linteo*, 8.
combeth him with a *Comb*,	pectit *Pectine*, 9.
9. and curleth him	crispat
with a *Crisping Iron*, 10.	*Calamistro*, 10.
Sometimes he cutteth a	Interdum secat Venam
Vein with a *Pen-knife*, 11.	*Scalpello*, 11.
where the Blood spirteth	ubi Sanguis propullulat,
out, 12.	12.

The *Chirurgeon* cureth *Wounds*.	*Chirurgus* curat *Vulnera*.

The Stable. LXXVII. Equile.

The *Horse-keeper*, 1. cleaneth the *Stable* from *Dung*, 2.	*Stabularias* (Equiso), 1. purgat *Stabulum* a *Fimo*, 2.
He tyeth a *Horse*, 3. with a *Halter*, 4. to the *Manger*, 5. or if he apt to bite, he maketh him fast with a *Muzzle*, 6.	Alligat *Equum*, 3. *Capistro*, 4. ad *Præsepe*, 5. aut si mordax constringit *Fiscella*, 6.
Then he streweth *Litter*, 7. under him.	Deinde substernit *Stramenta*, 7.
He *winnoweth Oats* with a *Van*, 8. (being mixt with Chaff, and taken out of a *Chest*, 10.) and with them feedeth the Horse, as also with *Hay*, 9.	*Ventilat Avenam*, *Vanno*, 8. (Paleis mixtam, ac depromptam à *Cista Pabulatoria*, 10.) câque pascit equum, ut & *Fœno*, 9.

Afterwards he leadeth	Postea ducit
him to the *Watering-trough*,	ad *Aquarium*, 11.
11. to water.	aquatum.
Then he rubbeth him	Tum detergit
with a *Cloth*, 12.	*Panno*, 12.
combeth him	depectit
with a *Curry-comb*, 15.	*Strigili*, 15.
covereth him	insternit
with an *Housing-cloth*, 14.	*Gausape*, 14.
and looketh upon his *Hoofs*	& inspicit *Soleas*,
whether the *Shoes*, 13.	an *Calcei ferrei*, 13.
be fast with the *Nails*.	firmis *Clavis* hæreant.

Dials. LXXVII. Horologia.

A *Dial*	*Horologium*
measureth Hours.	dimetitur Horas.
A *Sun-dial*, 1.	*Solarium*, 1.
sheweth by the shadow	ostendit umbrâ
of the *Pin*, 2.	*Gnomonis*, 2.
what a *Clock* it is;	quota sit *Hora*;
either on a Wall,	sive in Pariete,
or a *Compass*, 3,	sive in *Pyxide Magnetica*, 3.
An *Hour-glass*, 4.	*Clepsydra*, 4.

sheweth the four parts of an hour by the running of *Sand*, heretofore of water.

A *Clock*. 5. numbereth also the Hours of the Night, by the turning of the Wheels, the greatest whereof is drawn by a *Weight*, 6. and draweth the rest.

Then either the *Bell*, 7. by its sound, being struck on by the *Hammer*, or the *Hand*, 8. without, by its motion about sheweth the hour.

ostendit partes horæ quatuor, fluxu *Arenæ*, olim aquæ.

Automaton, 5. numerat etiam Nocturnas Horas, circulatione Rotarum, quarum maxima trahitur à *Pondere*, 6. & trahit cæteras.

Tum vel *Campana*, 7. sonitu suo, percussâ a *Malleolo*, vel *Index* extra Circuitione sua indicat horam.

The Picture. LXXIX, Pictura.

Pictures, 1. delight the Eyes and adorn Rooms.

The *Puinter*, 2. painteth an *Image*

Picturæ, 1. oblectant Oculos & ornant Conclavia.

Pictor, 2. pingit *Effigiem*

with a *Pencil*, 3.
in a *Table*, 4.
upon a *Case-frame*, 5.
holding his *Pollet*, 6. in his
left hand,
on which are the *Paints*
which were ground by the
Boy, 7. on a *Marble*.
The *Carver*
and *Statuary*
carve *Statues*, 8.
of Wood and Stone.
The *Graver*
and the *Cutter*
grave *Shapes*, 10.
and *Characters*
with a *Graving Chesil*, 9.
in Wood, Brass,
and other Metals.

Penicilio, 3.
in *Tabula*, 4.
super *Pluteo*, 5.
tenens *Orbem Pictorium*, 6.
in sinistra,
in quo *Pigmenta*
quæ terebantur à
puero, 7. in *marmore*.
Sculptor,
& *Statuarius*
exsculpunt *Statuas*, 8.
è Ligno & Lapide.
Cœlator
& *Scalptor*
insculpit *Figuras*, 10.
& *Characteres*,
Cælo, 9.
Ligno, Æri,
aliisque Metallis.

Looking-glasses. LXXX. Specularia.

Looking-glasses, 1. | *Specularia*, 1.

are provided that Men
may see themselves.
Spectacles, 2.
that he may see better,
who hath a weak sight.
Things afar off are seen
in a *Perspective Glass*, 3.
as things near at hand.
A *Flea* appeareth
in a *muliplying-glass*, 4.
like a little hog.
The Rays of the Sun,
burn wood
through a *Burning-glass*, 5.

parantur, ut homines
intueantur seipsos.
Perspicilla, 2.
ut cernat acius
qui habet visum debilem.
Remota videntur
per *telescopium*, 3.
ut proxima.
Pulex, 4.
in *Microscopio* apparet
ut porcellus.
Radii Solis
accendunt ligna
per *Vitrum urens*, 5.

The Cooper. LXXXI. Vietor.

The *Cooper*, 1.
having an *Apron*, 2, tied
about him,
maketh *Hoops*
of *Hazel-rods*, 3.
upon a *cutting-block*, 4.
with a *Spoke-Shave*, 5.

Vietor, 1.
amictus *Præcinctorio*, 2.
facit *Circulos*,
è *Virgis Colurnis*, 3.
super *Sellam incisoriam*, 4.
Scalpro bimanubriato, 5.

and *Lags*, 6. of *Timber*,	& *Assulas*, 6. ex *Ligno*.
Of *Lags* he maketh *Hogs-heads*, 7. and *Pipes*, 8.	Ex Assulis conficit *Dolia*, 7. & *Cupas*, 8.
with two *Heads*;	*Fundo* bino;
and *Tubs*, 9.	tum *Lacus*, 9.
Soes, 10.	*Labra*, 10.
Flaskets, 11.	*Pitynas* [Trimodia], 11.
Buckets, 12.	& *Situlas*, 12.
with one Bottom.	fundo uno.
Then he bindeth them with *Hoops*, 13.	Postea vincit *Circulis*, 13.
which he tyeth fast with small *Twigs*, 15.	quos ligat *Viminibus*, 15.
by means of a *Cramp-iron*, 14.	ope *Falcis vietoriæ*, 14.
and he fitteth them on with a *Mallet*, 16.	& aptat *Tudite*, 16.
and a *Driver*, 17.	ac *Tudicula*, 17.

LXXXII.

The Roper, and the Cordwainer.

Restio, & Lorarius.

The *Roper*, 1.	*Restio*, 1.

twisteth *Cords*, 2.	contorquet *Funes*, 2.
of *Tow*, or *Hemp*, 4.	è *Stupa*, 4. vel *Cannabi*,
(which he wrappeth about	quam circumdat
himself) by	sibi
the turning of a *Wheel*, 3.	agitatione *Rotulæ*, 3.
Thus are made	Sic fiunt,
first *Cords*, 5.	primò *Funiculi*, 5.
then *Ropes*, 6.	tum *Restes*, 6.
and at last, *Cables*, 7.	tandem *Rudentes*, 7.
The *Cord-wainer*, 8.	*Lorarius*, 8.
cutteth great *Thongs*, 10.	scindit *Loramenta*, 10.
Bridles, 11.	*Fræna*, 11.
Girdles, 12.	*Cingula*, 12.
Sword-belts, 13.	*Baltheos*, 13.
Pouches, 14.	*Crumenas*, 14.
Port-mantles, 15. &c.	*Hippoperas*, 15., &c.
out of a *Beast-hide*, 9.	de *corio bubulo*, 9.

The Traveller. LXXXIII. Viator.

A *Traveller*, 1.	*Viator*, 1.
beareth on his shoulders	portat humeris

in a *Budget*, 2.
those things
which his *Satchel*, 3.
or *Pouch*, 4. cannot hold.
He is covered
with a *Cloak*, 5.
He holdeth a *Staff*, 6. in
his hand wherewith
to bear up himself.
He hath need of
Provision for the way,
as also of a pleasant and
merry *Companion*, 7.
Let him not forsake the
High-road, 9. for a *Foot-way*, 8. unless it be a
beaten Path.
By-ways, 10.
and *places where two ways meet*, 11.
deceive and lead men aside
into *uneven-places*, 12.
so do not *By-paths*, 13.
and *Cross-ways*, 14.
Let him therefore en-
quire of *those he meeteth*,
15. which way he must go;
and let him take heed
of *Robbers*, 16.
as in the *way*, so also
in the *Inn*, 17. where
he lodgeth all Night.

in *Bulga*, 2.
quæ non capit
Funda, 3.
vel *Marsupium*, 4.
Tegitur
Lacernâ, 5.
Tenet *Baculum*, 6. Manu
quo
se fulciat.
Opus habet
Viatico,
ut & fido & facundo
Comite, 7.
Non deserat *Viam*
regiam propter *Semitam*, 8.
nisi sit
Callis tritus.
Avia, 10.
& *Bivia*, 11.
fallunt & seducunt,
in *Salebras*, 12.
non æquè *Tramites*, 13.
& *Compita*, 14.
Sciscitet igitur
obvios, 15.
quà sit eundum;
& caveat
Prædones, 16.
ut in *viâ*, sic etiam
in *Diversorio*, 17.
ubi pernoctat.

The Horse-man. LXXXIV. Eques.

The *Horse-man*, 1. setteth a *Saddle*, 2. on his *Horse*, 3. and girdeth it on with a *Girth*, 4.	*Eques*, 1. imponit *Equo*, 2. *Ephippium*, 3. idque succingit *Cingulo*, 4.
He layeth a *Saddle-cloth*, 5. also upon him.	Insternit etiam *Dorsuale*, 5.
He decketh him with *Trappings*, a *Fore-stall*, 6. a *Breast-cloth*, 7. and a *Crupper*, 8.	Ornat eum *Phaleris*, *Frontali*, 6. *Antilena*, 7. & *Postilena*, 8.
Then he getteth upon his Horse, putteth his feet into the *Stirrops*, 9. taketh the *Bridle-rein*, 10. 11. in his left hand, wherewith he guideth and holdeth the Horse.	Deinde insilit in Equum, indit pedes *Stapedibus*, 9. capessit *Lorum* (habenam), 10. *Freni*, 11. sinistrâ quo flectit, & retinet Equum.
Then he putteth to his *Spurs*, 12.	Tum admovet *Calcaria*, 12.

and setteth him on with a *Switch*, 13. and holdeth him in with a *Musrol*, 14.

incitatque *Virgula*, 13. & coërcet *Postomide*, 14.

The *Holsters*, 15. hang down from the *Pummel* of the *Saddle*, 16. in which the *Pistols*, 17. are put.

Bulgæ, 15. pendent ex *Apice Ephippii*, 16. quibus *Sclopi*, 17. inseruntur.

The Rider is clad in a short *Coat*, 18. his *Cloak* being tyed behind him, 19.

Ipse Eques induitur *Chlamyde*, 18. *Lacernâ* revinctâ, 19. â tergo.

A *Post*, 20. is carried on Horseback at full Gallop.

Veredarius, 20. fertur Equo cursim.

Carriages. LXXXV Vehicula.

We are carried on a *Sled*, 1. over Snow and Ice.

Vehimur *Trahâ*, 1. super Nivibus & Glacie.

A Carriage with one Wheel, is called a *Wheelbarrow*, 2.

Vehiculum unirotum, dicitur *Pabo*, 2.

with two Wheels, a *Cart*, 3.
with four Wheels, a *Wagon*,
which is either
a *Timber-wagon*, 4.
or a *Load-wagon*, 5.

The parts of the Wagon
are, the *Neep* (or draught-
tree), 6. the *Beam*, 7.
the *Bottom*, 8.
and the *Sides*, 9.

Then the *Axle-trees*, 10.
about which the *Wheels*
run, the *Lin-pins*, 11.
and *Axletree-staves*, 12. being fastened before them.

The *Nave*, 13. is the
groundfast of the *Wheel*,
14. from which come
twelve *Spokes*, 15.

The *Ring* encompasseth
these, which is made
of six *Felloes*, 16.
and as many *Strakes*, 17.
Hampiers and *Hurdles*, 18.
are set in a Wagon.

birotum, *Carrus*, 3.
quadrirotum, *Currus*,
qui vel
Sarracum, 4.
vel *Plaustrum*, 5.

Partes Currûs sunt,
Temo, 6.
Jugum, 7.
Compages, 8.
Spondæ, 9.

Tum *Axes*, 10.
circa quos *Rotæ* currunt,
Paxillis, 11.
& *Obicibus*, 12.
præfixis.

Modiolus, 13. est
Basis *Rotæ*, 14.
ex quo prodeunt
duodecim *Radii*, 15.

Orbile ambit hos,
compositum
è sex *Absidibus*, 16.
& totidem *Canthis*, 17.
Corbes & *Crates*, 18.
imponuntur Currui.

LXXXVI.

Carrying to and fro. — **Vectura.**

The *Coach-man*, 1.
joineth a *Horse fit to match*
a Saddle-horse, 2, 3.
to the *Coach-tree*,
with *Thongs* or *Chains*, 5.
hanging down from the
Collar, 4.

Then he sitteth upon
the *Saddle-horse*,
and driveth them that go
before him, 6.
with a *Whip*, 7.
and guideth them
with a *String*, 8

He greaseth the *Axle-tree*
with *Axle-tree grease*
out of a *Grease-pot*, 9.
and stoppeth the wheel
with a *Trigen*, 10.

Auriga, 1.
jungit *Parippum*, 2. *Sellario*, 3.
ad *Temonem*,
Loris vel *Catenis*, 5.
dependentibus
de *Helcio*, 4.

Deinde insidet
Sellario,
agit ante se antecessores, 6.
Scuticâ, 7.
& flectit
Funibus, 8.

Ungit *Axem*
Axungiâ,
ex *vase unguentorio*, 9.
& inhibet rotam
Sufflamine, 10.

in a steep descent.
And thus the Coach is driven along the *Wheel-ruts*, 11.
Great Persons are carryed *with six Horses*, 12.
by two *Coachmen*,
in a Hanging-wagon,
which is called
a *Coach*, 13.
Others *with two Horses*, 14. in a *Chariot*, 15.
Horse Liiters, 16, 17.
are carried by two Horses.
They use
Pack-Horses,
instead of *Waggons*,
thorow *Hills* that are not passable, 18.

in præcipiti descensu.
Et sic aurigatur
per *Orbitas*, 11.
Magnates vehuntur
Sejugibus, 12.
duobus *Rhedariis*,
Curru pensili,
qui vocatur
Carpentum (Pilentum), 13.
Alii *Bijugibus*, 14.
Essedo, 15.
Arceræ, 16. & *Lacticæ*, 17.
portantur à duobus Equis.
Utuntur
Jumentis Clitellariis,
loco *Curruum*,
per *montes* invios, 18.

LXXXVII.

Passing over Waters. — **Transitus Aquarum**

Lest he that is to pass over a River should be wet,

Trajecturus flumen ne madefiat,

Bridges, 1.	*Pontes*, 1.
were invented for Carriages, and *Foot-bridges*, 2.	excogitati sunt pro Vehiculis & *Ponticuli*, 2.
for Foot-men.	pro Peditibus.
If a river	Si Flumen
have a *Foord*, 3.	habet *Vadum*, 3.
it *is waded over*, 4.	*vadatur*, 4.
Flotes, 5. also are made of Timber pinned together;	*Rates*, 5. etiam struuntur ex compactis tignis:
or *Ferry-boats*, 6.	vel *Pontones*, 6.
of planks laid close together for fear they should receive Water.	ex trabibus consolidatis, ne excipiant aquam.
Besides *Scullers*, 7.	Porrò *Lintres* (Lembi), 7.
are made, which are rowed	fabricantur, qui
with an *Oar*, 8.	aguntur *Remo*, 8.
or *Pole*, 9.	vel *Conto*, 9.
or haled	aut trahuntur
with an *Haling-rope*, 10.	*Remulco*, 10.

Swimming. LXXXVIII. Natatus.

Men are wont also	Solent etiam
to swim over Waters	tranare aquas

upon a *bundle of flags*, 1.
and besides upon blown
Beast-bladders, 2.
and after, by throwing
their *Hands* and *Feet*, 3.
abroad.

super *scirpeum fascem*, 1.
porrò super inflatas *boum*
Vesicas, 2.
deinde liberè jactatu
Manuum Pedumque, 3.

And at last they learned
to tread the water, 4.
being plunged up to the
girdle-stead, and carrying
their Cloaths upon their
head.

Tandem didicerunt
calcare aquam, 4.
immersi
cingulo tenus & gestantes
Vestes supra caput.

A *Diver*, 5.
can swim also under
the water like a Fish.

Urinator, 5.
etiam natare potest
sub aquâ, ut Piscis.

A Galley. LXXXIX. Navis actuaria.

A *Ship* furnished
with *Oars*, 1.
is a *Barge*, 2.
or a *Foyst*, &c.
in which the *Rowers*, 3.

Navis instructa
Remis, 1.
est *Uniremis*, 2.
vel *Biremis*, &c.
in quâ *Remiges*, 3.

sitting on *Seats*, 4.	considentes pre *Transtra*,
by the *Oar-rings*,	4. ad *Scalmos*,
row, by striking the water	remigant pellendo aquam
with the *Oars*, 5.	*Remis*,
The *Ship-master*, 6.	*Proreta*, 6.
standing in the *Fore-castle*,	stans in *Prora*,
and the *Steers-man*, 7.	& *Gubernator*, 7.
sitting at the *Stern*,	sedens in *Puppi*,
and holding the *Rudder*, 8.	tenensque *Clavum*, 8.
steer the *Vessel*.	gubernant *Navigium*.

A Merchant-ship. XC. Navis oneraria.

A *Ship*, 1.	*Navigium*, 1.
is driven onward	impellitur,
not by Oars, but by the	non remis, sed
only force of the Winds.	solâ vi Ventorum.
In it is a *Mast*, 2. set up,	In illo *Malus*, 2. erigi-
fastened with *Shrowds*, 3.	tur, firmatus *Funibus*, 3.
on all sides to the *main-*	undique ad *Oras Navis*,
chains.	

to which the *Sail-yards*, 4.	cui annectuntur *Antennæ*, 4.
are tied, and the *Sails*, 5. to	his, *Vela*, 5. quæ
these, which are *spread*	*expanduntur*, 6.
open, 6. to the wind, and	ad Ventum
are hoysed by *Bowlings*, 7.	& *Versoriis*, 7. versantur.
The Sails are	Vela sunt
the *Main-sail*, 8.	*Artemon*, 8.
the *Trinket*, or *Fore-sail*, 9.	*Dolon*, 9.
the *Misen-sail* or *Poop-sail*, 10.	& *Epidromus*, 10.
The *Beak*, 11.	*Rostrum*, 11.
is in the *Fore-deck*.	est in *Prora*.
The *Ancient*, 12.	*Signum* (vexillum), 12.
is placed in the *Stern*.	ponitur in *Puppi*.
On the Mast	In Malo
is the *Foretop*, 13.	est *Corbis*, 13.
the *Watch-tower* of the Ship	*Specula* Navis
and over the *Fore-top*	& supra *Galeam*
a *Vane*, 14.	*Aplustre*, 14.
to shew which way the Wind standeth.	Ventorum Index.
The ship is stayed	Navis sistitur
with an *Anchor*, 15.	*Anchorâ*, 15.
The depth is fathomed	Profunditas exploratur
with a *Plummet*, 16.	*Bolide*, 16.
Passengers walk up and	Navigantes deambulant
down the *Decks*, 17.	in *Tabulato*, 17.
The Sea men run to and	Nautæ cursitant
fro through the *Hatches*, 18.	per *Foros*, 18.
And thus, even Seas	Atque ita, etiam Maria
are passed over.	trajiciuntur.

Ship-wreck. XCI. Naufragium.

When a *Storm*, 1. ariseth on a sudden, they strike *Sail*, 2. lest the Ship should be dashed against *Rocks*, 3 or light upon *Shelves*, 4.	Cum *Procella*, 1. oritur repentè contrahunt *Vela*, 2. ne Navis ad *Scopulos*, 3. allidatur, aut incidat in *Brevia* (Syrtes), 4.
If they cannot hinder her they suffer *Ship-wreck*, 5.	Si non possunt prohibere patiuntur *Naufragium*, 5.
And then the men, the *Wares*, and all things are miserably lost.	Tum Homines, *Merces*, omnia miserabiliter pereunt.
Nor doth the *Sheat-anchor*, 6 being cast with a *Cable*, do any good.	Neque hic *Sacra anchora*, 6. *Rudenti* jacta quidquam adjuvat.
Some escape, either on a *Plank*, 7. and by swimming, or in the *Boat*, 8.	Quidam evadunt, vel *tabula*, 7. ac enatando, vel *Scapha*, 8.
Part of the Wares, with the dead folks, is carried out of the *Sea*, 9. oupn the Shoars.	Pars Mercium cum mortuis a *Mari*, 9. in littora defertur.

Writing. XCII. Ars Scriptoria.

The Ancients writ	Veteres scribebant
in *Tables done over with wax*	in *Tabellis ceratis*
with a brazen *Poitrel*, 1.	æneo *Stilo*, 1.
with the *sharp end*, 2.	cujus *parte cuspidata*, 2.
whereof letters were en-	exarabantur literæ,
graven and rubbed out	rursum vero obliteraban-
again with the *broad end*, 3.	tur *planâ*.
Afterwards	Deinde
they writ *Letters*	*Literas* pingebant
with a *small Reed*, 4.	*subtili Calamo*, 4.
We use a *Goose-quill*, 5.	Nos utimur *Anserina Pen-*
the *Stem*, 6.	*na*, 5. cujus *Caulem*, 6.
of which we make	temperamus
with a *Pen-knife*, 7.	*Scalpello*, 7.
then we dip the *Neb*	tum intingimus *Crenam*
in an *Ink-horn*, 8.	in *Atramentario*, 8.
which is stopped	quod obstruitur
with a *Stopple*, 9.	*Operculo*, 9.
and we put our *Pens*,	& *Pennas* recondimus
into a *Pennar*, 10.	in *Calamario*, 10.
We dry a Writing	Siccamus Scripturam

with *Blotting-paper*,
or *Calis-sand*
out of a *Sand-box*, 11.
And we indeed
write from the left hand
towards the right, 12.
the *Hebrews*
from the right hand
towards the left, 13.
the *Chinese* and other *Indians*, from the top downwards, 14.

Chartâ bibulâ,
vel *Arenâ scriptoria*,
ex *Theca Pulveraria*, 11.
Et nos quidem
scribimus â sinistra
dextrorsum, 12.
Hebræi
â dextrâ
sinistrorsum, 13.
Chinenses & *Indi* alii,
â summo deorsum, 14.

Paper. XCIII. Papyrus.

The Ancients used
Beech-Boards, 1.
or *Leaves*, 2.
as also *Barks*, 3. of *Trees*;
especially
of an Egyptian Shrub,
which was called *Papyrus*.
Now *Paper* is in use
which the *Paper-maker*

Veteres utebantur
Tabulis Faginis, 1.
aut *Foliis*, 2.
ut & *Libris*, 3. *Arborum*;
præsertim
Arbusculæ Ægyptiæ,
cui nomen erat *Papyrus*.
Nunc *Charta* est in usu,
quam *Chattopœus*

maketh in a *Paper-mill*, 4.	in *mola Papyracea*,4. confic-
of *Linen rags*, 5.	it è *Linteis vetustis*, 5.
stamped to *Mash*, 6.	in *Pulmentum* contusis, 6.
which being taken up in	quod haustum
Frames, 7.	*Normulis*, 7.
he spreadeth into *Sheets*, 8.	diducit in *Plagulas*, 8.
and setteth them in the Air	exponitque aëri,
that they may be dryed.	ut siccentur.
Twenty-five of these	Harum XXV.
make a *Quire*, 9.	faciunt *Scapum*, 9.
twenty Quires a *Ream*, 10.	XX. Scapi *Volumen minus*,
and ten of these	10. horum X.
a *Bale of Paper*, 11.	*Volumen majus*, 11.
That which is to last	Duraturum diu
long is written on *Parch-*	scribitur in *Mem-*
ment, 12.	*brana*, 12.

Printing. XCIV. Typographia.

The *Printer* hath	*Typographus* habet
metal Letters	*Typos* Metallos,
in a large number	magno numero dis-
put into *Boxes*, 5.	tributos per *Loculamenta*,5.
The *Compositor*, 1.	*Typotheta*, 1.

taketh them out one by one	eximit illos singulatim,
and according to the *Copy*,	& secundum *exemplar*,
(which he hath fastened	(quod habet præfixum
before him in a *Visorum*, 2.)	sibi *Retinaculo*, 2.)
composeth words	componit Verba
in a *Composing-stick*, 3.	*Gnomone*, 3.
till a *Line* be made;	donec *versus* fiat;
he putteth these in a *Gally*,	hos indit *Formæ*, 4.
4. till a *Page*, 6. be made,	donec *Pagina*, 6. fiat;
and these again in a *Form*,	has iterum *Tabulâ compos-*
7. and he locketh them up	*itoriâ*, 7. coarctaque eos
in *Iron Chases*, 8.	*Marginibus ferreis*, 8.
with *Coyns*, 9.	ope *Cochlearum*, 9.
lest they should drop out,	ne dilabantur,
and putteth them under	ac subjicit
the *Press*, 10.	*Prelo*, 10.
Then the *Press-man*	Tum *Impressor*
beateth it over	illinit
with *Printers Ink*,	*Atramento impressorio*
by means of *Balls*, 11.	ope *Pilarum*, 11.
spreadeth upon it the Pa-	super imponit Chartas
pers put in the *Frisket*, 12.	inditas *Operculo*, 12.
which being put	quas subditas
under the *Spindle*, 14.	*Trochleæ*, 14.
on the *Coffin*, 13.	in *Tigello*, 13.
and pressed down with a	& impressas
Bar, 15. he maketh	*Suculâ*, 15. facit
to take impression.	imbibere typos.

XCV.

The Booksellers Shop. | Bibliopolium.

The *Bookseller*, 1	*Bibliopola*, 1.
selleth *Books*	vendit *Libros*
in a *Booksellers Shop*, 2.	in *Bibliopolio*, 2.
of which he writeth	quorum conscribit
a *Catalogue*, 3.	*Catalogum*, 3.
The Books are placed	Libri disponuntur
on *Shelves*, 4.	per *Repositoria*, 4.
and are laid open for use	& exponuntur ad usum,
upon a *Desk*, 5.	super *Pluteum*, 5.
A Multitude of Books	Multitudo Librorum
is called a *Library*, 6.	vocatur *Bibliotheca*, 6.

The Book-binder. XCVI. Bibliopegus.

In times past they glewed Paper to Paper, and rolled them up together into one *Roll*, 1.	Olim agglutinabant Chartam Chartæ, convolvebantque eas in unum *Volumen*, 1.
At this day the *Book-binder* bindeth Books, whilst he wipeth, 2. over Papers steept in *Gum-water*, and then foldeth them together, 3.	Hodiè *Compactor* compingit Libros, dum tergit, 2. chartas maceratas *aquâ glutinosâ*, deinde complicat, 3.
beatheth with a hammer, 4.	malleat, 4.
then stitcheth them up, 5.	tum consuit, 5.
presseth them in a *Press*, 6.	conprimit *Prelo*, 6.
which hath two *Screws*, 7.	quod habet duos *Cochleas*, 7.
glueth them on the back,	conglutinat dorso,
cutteth off the edges with a *round Knife*, 8.	demarginat rotundo *Cultro*, 8.
and at last covereth them with *Parchment* or *Leather*, 9.	tandem vestit *Membranâ* vel *Corio*, 9.
maketh them handsome,	efformat,
and setteth on *Clasps*, 10.	& affigit *Uncinulos*, 10.

A Book. XCVII. Liber.

A *Book*
as to its outward shape,
is either in *Folio*, 1.
or in *Quarto*, 2.
in *Octavo*, 3.
in *Duodecimo*, 4. either
made to open Side-wise, 5.
or *Long-wise*, 6.
with *Brazen Clasps*, 7.
or *Strings*, 8.
and *Square-bosses*, 9.

Within are *Leaves*, 10.
with two *Pages*,
sometimes divided with
Columns, 11.
and *Marginal Notes*, 12.

Liber,
quoad exteriorem formam
est vel in *Folia*, 1.
vel in *Quarto*, 2.
in *Octavo*, 3.
in *Duodecimo*, 4.
vel *Columnatus*, 5.
vel *Linguatus*, 6.
cum *Æneis Clausuris*, 7.
vel *Ligulis*, 8.
& *angularibus Bullis*, 9.

Intùs sunt *Folia*, 10.
duabis *Paginis*,
aliquando *Columnis*, 11. divisa cumq;
Notis Marginalibus, 12.

A School. XCVIII. Schola.

A *School*, 1.
is a Shop in which
Young Wits are fashion'd
to vertue, and it is
distinguish'd into *Forms*.
The *Master*, 2.
sitteth in a *Chair*, 3.
the *Scholars*, 4.
in *Forms*, 5.
he teacheth, they learn.
Some things
are writ down before them
with *Chalk* on a *Table*, 6.
Some sit
at a Table, and write, 7.
he mendeth their Faults, 8.
Some stand and rehearse
things committed to
memory, 9.
Some talk together, 10.
and behave themselves
wantonly and carelessly;

Schola, 1.
est Officina, in quâ
Novelli Animi formantur
ad virtutem, &
distinguitur in *Classes*.
Præceptor, 2.
sedet in *Cathedra*, 3.
Discipuli, 4.
in *Subselliis*, 5.
ille docet, hi discunt.
Quædam
præscribuntur illis
Cretâ in *Tabella*, 6.
Quidam sedent
ad Mensam, & scribunt, 7.
ipse corrigit Mendas, 8.
Quidam stant, & reci-
tant mandata
memoriæ, 9.
Quidam confabulantur,
10. ac gerunt se
petulantes, & negligentes;

these are chastised	hi castigantur
with a *Ferrula*. 11.	*Ferulâ* (baculo), 11.
and a *Rod*, 12.	& *Virgâ*, 12.

The Study. XCIX. Museum.

The *Study*, 1.	*Museum*, 1.
is a place where a Student,	est locus ubi Studiosus, 2.
2. apart from Men,	secretus ab Hominibus,
sitteth alone,	sedet solus
addicted to his *Studies*,	deditus *Studiis*,
whilst he readeth *Books*, 3.	dum lectitat *Libros*, 3.
which being within his	quos penes se
reach he layeth open up-	& exponit super
on a *Desk*, 4. and picketh	*Pluteum*, 4. & excerpit
all the best things out of	optima quæque ex illis
them into his own *Manual*,	in *Manuale* suum, 5.
5. or marketh them in	notat in illis
them with a *Dash*, 6.	*Liturâ*, 6.
or a *little Star*, 7.	vel *Asterisco*, 7.
in the *Margent*.	ad *Margiem*.
Being to sit up late,	Lucubraturus,

he setteth a *Candle*, 8. on a *Candlestick*, 9. which is snuffed with *Snuffers*, 10. before the Candle, he placeth a *Screen*, 11. which is green, that it may not hurt his eye-sight; richer Persons use a *Taper*, for a *Tallow-candle* stinketh and smoaketh.

A *Letter*, 12. is wrapped up, writ upon, 13. and sealed, 14.

Going abroad by night, he maketh use of a *Lanthorn*, 15. or a *Torch*, 16.

elevat *Lychnum* (*Canelam*), 8. in *Candelabra*, 9. qui emungitur *Emunctorio*, 10. ante Lynchum collocat *Umbraculum*, 11. quod viride est, ne hebetet oculorum aciem; opulentiores utuntur *Cereo* nam *Candela sebacea* fœtet & fugimat.

Epistola, 12. complicatur, inscribitur, 13. & obsignatur, 14.

Prodiens noctu utitur *Lanterna*, 15. vel *Face*, 16.

C.

Arts belonging to Speech.

Artes Sermones.

Grammar, 1.

Grammatica, 1.

is conversant about *Letters*, 2. of which it maketh *Words*, 3. and teacheth how to utter, write, 4. put together and part them rightly.

Rhetorick, 5.
doth as it were paint, 6.
a rude form, 7.
of Speech with *Oratory Flourishes*, 8.
such as are *Figures*,
Elegancies,
Adagies,
Apothegms,
Sentences,
Similies,
Hierogylphicks, &c.

Poetry, 9.
gathereth these *Flowers of Speech*, 10.
and tieth them as it were
into a little *Garland*, 11.
and so making of *Prose*
a *Poem*,
it maketh several sorts of
Verses and *Odes*,
and is therefore crowned
with a *Laurel*, 12.

Musick, 13.
setteth *Tunes*, 14.
with *pricks*,
to which it setteth words,
and so singeth alone,
or in *Consort*,
or by Voice, or
Musical Instruments, 15.

versatur circa *Literas*, 2. ex quibus componit *Voces*, *verba*, 3. docetque eloqui, scribere, 4. construere, distinguere (interpungere) eas recte.

Rhetorica, 5.
pingit, 6. quasi
rudem *formam*, 7.
Sermonis *Oratoriis Pigmentis*, 8.
ut sunt *Figuræ*,
Elegantiæ,
Adagia (proverbia)
Apothegmata,
Sententiæ (Gnomæ)
Similia,
Hieroglyphica, &c.

Poesis, 9.
colligit hòs *Flores Orationis*, 10.
& colligat quasi
in *Corallam*, 11.
atque ita, faciens è *prosa*
ligatam orationem,
componi varia
Carmina & *Hymnos* (*Odas*)
ac propterea coronatur
Lauru, 12.

Musica, 13.
componit *Melodias*, 14.
Notis,
quibus aptat verba,
atque ita cantat sola
vel *Concentu* (*Symphonia*),
aut voce aut
Instrumentis Musicis, 15.

Musical Instruments. CI. Instrumenta musica.

Musical Instruments are those which make a sound:	*Musica instrumenta* sunt quæ edunt vocem :
First,	Primò,
when they are beaten upon,	cum pulsantur,
as a *Cymbal*, 1. with a *Pestil*,	ut *Cymbalum*, 1. *Pistillo*,
a *little Bell*, 2.	*Tintinnabulum*, 2.
with an *Iron pellet* within;	intus *Globulo ferreo*,
or *Rattle*, 3.	*Crepitaculum*, 3.
by tossing it about:	circumversando;
a *Jews-Trump*, 4.	*Crembalum*, 4.
being put to the mouth,	ori admotum,
with the fingers;	Digito;
a *Drum*, 5.	*Tympanum*, 5.
and a *Kettle*, 6.	& *Ahenum*, 6.
with a *Drum-stick*, 7.	*Claviculâ*, 7.
as also the *Dulcimer*, 8.	ut & *Sambuca*, 8.
with the *Shepherds-harp*, 9.	cum *Organo pastoritio*, 9.
and the *Tymbrel*, 10.	& *Sistrum* (Crotalum), 10.
Secondly,	Secundò,
upon which *strings* are stretched, and struck upon,	in quibus *Chordæ* intenduntur & plectuntur
as the *Psaltery*, 11.	ut *Nablium*, 11.

and the *Virginals*, 12.	cum *Clavircordio*, 12.
with both hands;	utrâque manu;
the *Lute*, 13.	*Testudo* (Chelys), 13.
(in which is the *Neck*, 14.	(in quâ *Jugum*, 14.
the *Belly*, 15,	*Magadium*, 15.
the *Pegs*, 16.	& *Verticilli*, 16.
by which the *Strings*, 17.	quibus *Nervi*, 17.
are stretched	intenduntur
upon the *Bridge*, 18.)	super *Ponticulam*, 18.)
the *Cittern*, 19.	& *Cythara*, 19.
with the right hand only,	Dexterâ tantum,
the *Vial*, 20.	*Pandura*, 20.
with a *Bow*, 21.	*Plectro*, 21.
and the *Harp*, 23.	& *Lyra*, 23.
with a Wheel within,	intus rotâ,
which is turned about:	quæ versatur:
the *Stops*, 22.	*Dimensiones*, 22.
in every one are touched	in singulis tanguntur
with the left hand.	sinistra.
At last,	Tandem
those which are blown,	quæ inflantur,
as with the mouth,	ut Ore,
the *Flute*, 24.	*Fistula* (*Tibia*), 24.
the *Shawm*, 25.	*Gingras*, 25.
the *Bag-pipe*, 26.	*Tibia utricularis*, 26.
the *Cornet*, 27.	*Lituus*, 27.
the *Trumpet*, 28, 29.	*Tuba*, 28. *Buccina*, 29.
or with *Bellows*,	vel *Follibus*, ut
as a *pair of Organs*, 30.	*Organum pneumaticum*, 30.

Philosophy. CII. Philosophia.

The *Naturalist*, 1.	*Physicus*, 1.
vieweth all the works of	speculatur omnia Dei
God in the World.	Opera in Mundo.
The *Supernaturalist*, 2.	*Metaphysicus*, 2.
searches out the *Causes*	perscrutatur *Causas*,
and *Effects* of things.	& rerum *Effecta*.
The *Arithmetician*,	*Arithmeticus*
reckoneth *numbers*,	computat *numeros*,
by adding, subtracting,	addendo, subtrahendo,
multiplying and dividing;	multiplicando, dividendo;
and that either by *Cyphers*,	idque vel *Cyphris*, 3.
3. on a *Slate*,	in *Palimocesto*,
or by *Counters*, 4.	vel *Calculis*, 4.
upon a *Desk*.	super *Abacum*.
Country people reckon, 5.	*Rustici* numerant, 5.
with *figures of tens*, X.	*Decussibus*, X.
and *figures of five*, V.	& *Quincuncibus*, V.
by *twelves*, *fifteens*,	per *Duodenas*, *Quindenas*,
and *threescores*.	& *Sexagenas*.

Geometry. CIII. Geometria.

A *Geometrician*
measureth the *height* of
a *Tower*, 1 . . . . 2.
or the *distance*
of *places*, 3 . . . . 4.
either with a *Quadrant*, 5.
or a *Jacob's-staff*, 6.
He maketh out the
Figures of things,
with *Lines*, 7.
Angles, 8.
and *Circles*, 9.
by a *Rule*, 10.
a *Square*, 11.
and a *pair of Compasses*, 12.
Out of these arise
an *Oval*, 13.
a *Triangle*, 14.
a *Quadrangle*, 15.
and other figures.

Geometra
metitur *Altitudinem*
Turris, 1 . . . . 2.
aut *distantiam*
Locorum, 3 . . . . 4.
sive *Quadrante*, 5.
sive *Radio*, 6.
Designat
Figuras rerum
Lineis, 7,
Angulis, 8.
& *Circulis*, 9.
ad *Regulam*, 10.
Normam. 11.
& *Circinum*, 12.
Ex his oriuntur
Cylindrus, 13.
Trigonus 14.
Tetragonus, 15.
& aliæ figuræ.

The Celestial Sphere. CIV. Sphera cælestis.

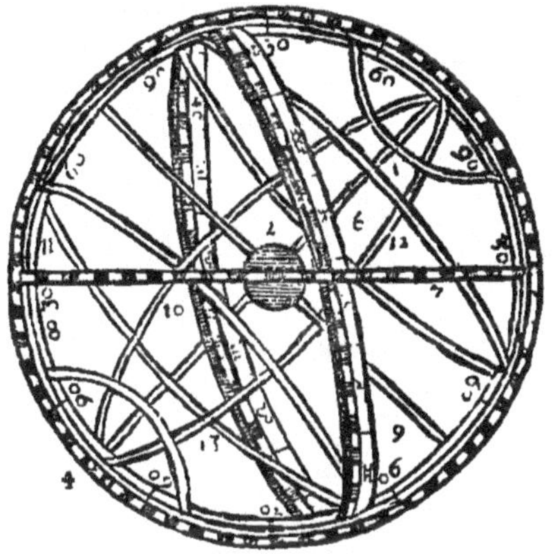

Astronomy considereth the *motion of the Stars*, *Astrology* the Effects of them.

The *Globe of Heaven* is turned about upon an *Axle-tree*, 1. about the *Globe of the Earth*, 2. in the space of XXIV. hours.

The *Pole-stars*, or *Pole*, the *Arctick*, 3. the *Antarctick*, 4. conclude the *Axle-tree* at both ends.

The *Heaven* is full of Stars every where.

There are reckoned above a *thousand fixed Stars*; but of *Constellations towards the North*, XXI. *towards the South*, XVI.

Astronomia considerat *motus Astrorum*, *Astrologia* eorum Effectus.

Globus Cæli volvitur super *Axem*, 1. circa *globum terræ*, 2. spacio XXIV. horarum.

Stellæ polares, *Arcticus*, 3. *Antarcticus*, 4. finiunt *Axem* utrinque.

Cælum est Stellatum undique.

Stellarum fixarum numerantur plus *mille*; *Siderum* verò *Septentrionarium*, XXI. *Meridionalium*, XVI.

Add to these the XII.	Adde *Signa*, XII.
signs of the *Zodiaque*, 5.	*Zodiaci*, 5.
every one XXX. degrees,	quodlibet graduum, XXX.
whose names are ♈ *Aries*	quorum nomina sunt
♉ *Taurus*, ♊ *Gemini*,	♈ *Aries*, ♉ *Taurus*, ♊ *Gem.*
♋ *Cancer*, ♌ *Leo*, ♍ *Virgo*,	♋ *Cancer*, ♌ *Leo*, ♍ *Virgo*,
♎ *Libra*, ♏ *Scorpius*,	♐ *Libra*, ♏ *Scorpius*,
♐ *Sagittarius*, ♑ *Capricor*,	♎ *Sagittarius*, ♑ *Capricorn*,
♒ *Aquarius*, ♓ *Pisces*.	♒ *Aquarius*, ♓ *Pisces*.
Under this move the	Sub hoc cursitant
seven *Wandring-stars*	*Stellæ errantes* VII.
which they call *Planets*,	quas vocant *Planetas*,
whose way is a circle in	quorum via est Circulvs,
the middle of the Zodiack,	in medio Zodiaci,
called the *Ecliptick*, 6.	dictus *Ecliptica*, 6.
Other Circles are	Alii Circuli sunt
the *Horizon*, 7.	*Horizon*, 7.
the *Meridian*, 8.	*Meridianus*, 8.
the *Æquator*, 9.	*Equator*, 9.
the two *Colures*, the	duo *Coluri*,
one of the *Equinocts*, 10.	alter *Æquinoxiorum*, 10.
(of the *Spring*	(*Verni*,
when the ☉ entreth into ♈;	quando ☉ ingreditur ♈;
Autumnal	*Autumnalis*,
when it entreth in ♎)	quando ingreditur ♎)
the other of the *Solstices*, 11.	alter *Solsticiorum*, 11.
(*of the Summer*,	(*Æstivi*,
when the ☉ entreth into ♋	quando ☉ ingreditur ♋;
of the *Winter*	*Hyberni*,
when it entreth into ♑)	quando ingreditur ♑)
the *Tropicks*,	duo *Tropici*,
the *Tropick of Cancer*, 12.	*Tr. Cancri*, 12.
the *Tropick of Capricorn*, 13.	*Tr. Capricorni*, 13.
and the two	& duo
Polar Circles, 14....15.	*Polares*, 14....15.

CIV.

The Aspects of the Planets.

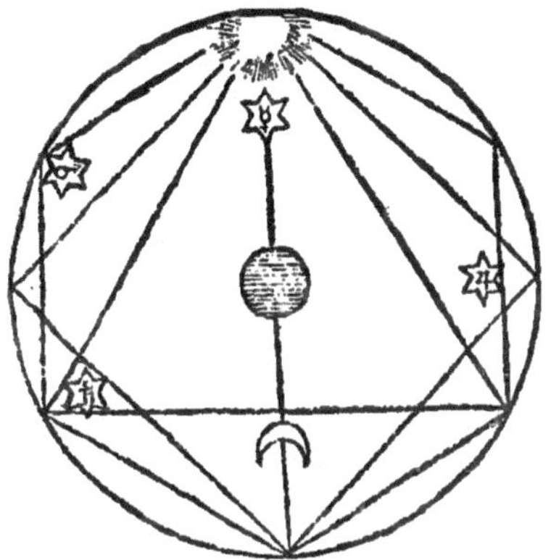

Planetarum Aspectus.

The *Moon* runneth through the *Zodiack* every *Month*.	*Luna* percurrit *Zodiacum* singulis *Mensibus*.
The *Sun*, ☉ in a Year.	*Sol*, ☉ Anno.
Mercury, ☿ and *Venus*, ♀ about the Sun, the one in a hundred and fifteen, the other in 585 days.	*Mercurius*, ☿ & *Venus*, ♀ circa Solem, illa CXV., hæc DLXXXV. Diebus.
Mars, ♂ in two years;	*Mars*, ♂ Biennio;
Jupiter, ♃ in almost twelve;	*Jupiter*, ♃ ferè duodecim;
Saturn, ♄ in thirty years.	*Saturnus*, ♄ triginta annis.
Hereupon they meet variously among themselves, and have mutual Aspects one towards another.	Hinc conveniunt variè inter se & se mutuo adspiciunt.

As here the ☉ and ☿ are in *Conjunction*.
☉ and *Moon* in *Opposition*,
☉ and ♄ in a *Trine Aspect*,
☉ and ♃ in a *Quartile*,
☉ and ♂ in a *Sextile*.

Ut hic sunt, ☉ & ☿ in *Conjunctione*,
☉ and *Luna* in *Oppositione*,
☉ & ♄ in *Trigono*,
☉ & ♃ in *Quadratura*,
☉ & ♂ in *Sextili*.

CV.

The Apparitions of the Moon.

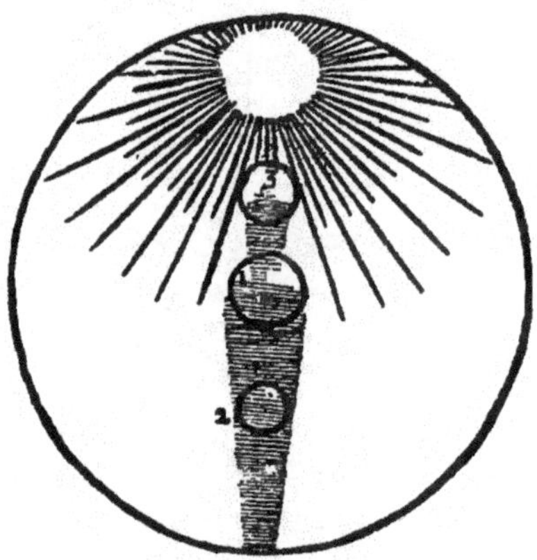

Phases Lunæ.

The *Moon* shineth not by her own *Light* but that which is borrowed of the *Sun*.

For the one half of it is always enlightned, the other remaineth darkish.

Hereupon we see it in *Conjunction* with the *Sun*, 1. to be obscure, almost none at all; in *Opposition*, 5.

Luna, lucet non sua propria *Luce*, sed mutuatâ a *Sole*.

Nam altera ejus medietas semper illuminatur, altera manet caliginosa.

Hinc videmus, in *Conjunctione Solis*, 1. obscuram, imo nullam: in *Oppositione*, 5.

whole and clear,	totam & lucidam,
(and we call it	(& vocamus
the *Full Moon* ;)	*Plenilunium* ;)
sometimes in the half,	alias dimidiam,
(and we call it the *Prime*, 3.	(& dicimus *Primam*, 3.
and *last Quarter*, 7.)	& *ultimam Quadram*, 7.)
Otherwise it waxeth, 2.. 4.	Cæteroqui crescit, 2..4.
or waneth, 6... 8.	aut decrescit, 6....8.
and is said to be *horned*,	& vocatur *falcata*,
or more than half *round*.	vel *gibbosa*.

The Eclipses. CVI. Eclipses.

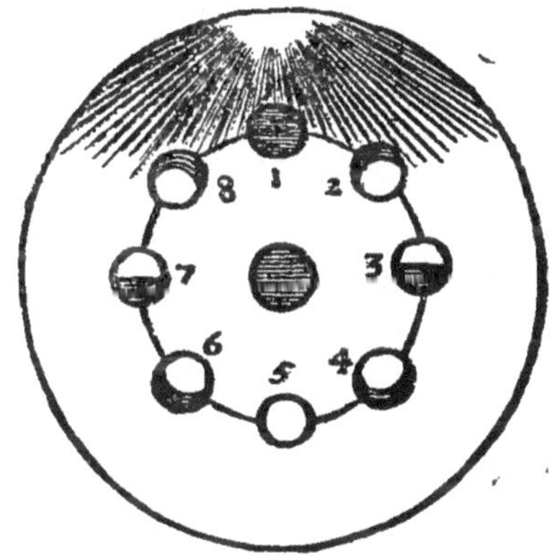

The *Sun*	*Sol*
is the fountain of light,	est fons Lucis,
inlightning all things,	illuminans omnia;
but the *Earth*, 1.	sed *Terra*, 1.
and the *Moon*, 2.	& *Luna*, 2.
being shady bodies, are not pierced with its rays, for they cast a shadow upon the place just over against them.	Corpora opaca, non penetrantur ejus radiis, nam jaciunt umbram in locum oppositum.
Therefore,	Ideo
when the Moon lighteth	cum Luna incidit

into the shadow of the *Earth*, 2. it is darkened, which we call an *Eclipse*, or defect.	in umbram *Terræ*, 2. obscuratur quod vocamus *Eclipsin* (deliquium) *Lunæ*.
But when the *Moon* runneth betwixt the *Sun* and the *Earth*, 3. it covereth it with its shadow; and this we call the *Eclipse* of the *Sun*, because it taketh from us the sight of the *Sun*, and its light; neither doth the *Sun* for all that suffer any thing, but the *Earth*.	Cum vero *Luna* currit inter *Solem* & *Terram*, 3. obtegit illum umbrâ suâ; & hoc vocamus *Eclipsin Solis*, quia adimit nobis prospectum *Solis*, & lucem ejus; nec tamen *Sol* patitur aliquid, sed *Terra*.

CVII. *a*

The terrestial Sphere.

Sphera terrestris.

The *Earth* is round, and therefore to be represented by two *Hemispheres*, a. . b.	*Terra* est rotunda, fingenda igitur duobus *Hemispheriis*, a. . b.
The Circuit of it	Ambitus ejus

is 360 *degrees*
(whereof every one maketh
60 *English* Miles
or 21600 Miles,)
and yet it is but a prick,
compared with the World,
whereof it is the *Centre*.

They measure Longitude of it by *Climates*, 1.
and the *Latitude*
by *Parallels*, 2.

The *Ocean*, 3. compasseth it about, and five *Seas* wash it, the *Mediterranean Sea*, 4. the *Baltick Sea*, 5. the *Red Sea*, 6. the *Persian Sea*, 7. and the *Caspian Sea*, 8.

est *graduum* CCCLX.
(quorum quisque facit
LX. Milliaria *Anglica*
vel 21600 Milliarium)
& tamen est punctum,
collata cum orbe,
cujus *Centrum* est.

Longitudinem ejus dimetiuntur *Climatibus*, 1.
Latitudinem,
lineis *Parallelis*, 2.

Oceanus, 3. ambit eam & *Maria* V. perfundunt *Mediterraneum*, 4. *Balticum*, 5. *Erythræum*, 6. *Persicum*, 7. *Caspium*, 8.

CVII. *b*

The terrestial Sphere.

Sphera terrestris.

It is divided into V. *Zones*, whereof the II. *frigid ones*, 9....9.

Distribuitur in *Zonas* V., quarum duæ *frigidæ*, 9....9.

are uninhabitable; the II. *Temperate* ones, 10 ..10. and the *Torrid* one, 11. habitable.	sunt inhabitabiles; duæ *Temperatæ*, 10....10. & *Torrida*, 11. habitantur.
Besides it is divided into three *Continents*; this of ours, 12. which is subdivided into *Europe*, 13. *Asia*, 14. *Africa*, 15. *America*, 16....16. (whose Inhabitants are *Antipodes* to us;) and the *South Land*, 17..17. yet unknown.	Ceterum divisa est in tres *Continentes*; nostram, 12. quæ subdividitur in *Europam*, 13. *Asiam*, 14. & *Africam*, 15. in *Americam*, 16....16. (cujus incolæ sunt *Antipodes* nobis;) & in *Terram Australem*, 17 ..17. adhuc incognitam.
They that dwell under the *Northpole*, 18. have the days and nights 6 months long.	Habitantes sub *Arcto*, 18. habent Dies Noctes semestrales,
Infinite *Islands* float in the Seas.	Infinitæ *Insulæ* natant in maribus.

Europe. CVIII. Europa.

The chief *Kingdoms* of *Europe*, are	In *Europâ* nostrâ sunt *Regna* primaria,

Spain, 1.	*Hispania*, 1.
France, 2.	*Gallia*, 2.
Italy, 3.	*Italia*, 3.
England, 4.	*Anglia* (Britania), 4.
Scotland, 5.	*Scotia*, 5.
Ireland, 6.	*Hibernia*, 6.
Germany, 7.	*Germania*, 7.
Bohemia, 8.	*Bohemia*, 8.
Hungary, 9.	*Hungaria*, 9.
Croatia, 10.	*Croatia*, 10.
Dacia, 11.	*Dacia*, 11.
Sclavonia, 12.	*Sclavonia*, 12.
Greece, 13.	*Græcia*, 13.
Thrace, 14.	*Thracia*, 14.
Podolia, 15.	*Podolia*, 15.
Tartary, 16.	*Tartaria*, 16.
Lituania, 17.	*Lituania*, 17.
Poland, 18.	*Polonia*, 18.
The *Netherlands*, 19.	*Belgium*, 19.
Denmark, 20.	*Dania*, 20.
Norway, 21.	*Norvegia*, 21.
Swethland, 22.	*Suecia*, 22.
Lapland, 23.	*Lappia*, 23.
Finland, 24.	*Finnia*, 24.
Lisland, 25.	*Livonia*, 25.
Prussia, 26.	*Borussia*, 26.
Muscovy, 27.	*Muscovia*, 27.
and *Russia*, 28.	*Russia*, 28.

Moral Philosophy. CIX. Ethica.

This *Life* is a *way*,
or a *place divided into two ways*, like
Pythagoras's Letter Y.
broad, 1.
on the left hand track;
narrow, 2. on the right;
that belongs to *Vice*, 3.
this to *Vertue*, 4.

Mind, Young Man, 5.
imitate *Hercules*:
leave the left hand way,
turn from Vice;
the *Entrance*, 6. is fair,
but the *End*, 7.
is ugly and steep down.

Go on the right hand,
though it be thorny, 8.
no way is unpassible to vertue; follow whither vertue leadeth

Vita hæc est *via*,
sive *Bivium*,
simile
Litteræ *Pithagoricæ* Y.
latum, 1.
sinistro tramite
angustum, 2. dextro;
ille *Vitii*, 3. est
hic *Virtutis*, 4.

Adverte juvenis, 5.
imitare *Herculem*;
linque sinistram,
aversare Vitium;
Aditus speciosus, 6.
sed *Exitus*, 7.
turpis & præceps.

Dextera ingredere,
utut spinosa, 8.
nulla via invia
virtuti; sequere quâ viâ
ducit virtus

through *narrow places* to *stately palaces*, to the *Tower of honour*, 9.	per *angusta*, ad *augusta*, ad *Arcem honoris*, 9.
Keep the middle and streight *path*, and thou shalt go very safe.	Tene medium & rectum *tramitem;* ibis tutissimus.
Take heed thou do not go too much on the right hand, 10.	Cave excedas ad dextram, 10.
Bridle in, 12. the wild Horse, 11. of Affection, lest thou fall down headlong.	Compesce freno, 12. equum ferocem, 11. Affectûs ne præceps fias.
See thou dost not go amiss on the left hand, 13. in an ass-like sluggishness, 14. but go onwards constantly, persevere to the end, and thou shalt be crown'd, 15.	Cave deficias ad sinistram, 13. segnitie asininâ, 14. sed progredere constanter pertende ad finem, & coronaberis, 15.

Prudence. CX. Prudentia.

Prudence, 1. looketh upon all things	*Prudentia*, 1. circumspectat omnia

as a *Serpent*, 2.
and doeth, speaketh, or thinketh nothing in vain.

She *looks backwards*, 3. as into a *Looking-glass*, 4. to *things past;* and seeth *before her*, 5. as with a *Perspective-glass*, 7. *things to come*, or the *End*, 6. and so she perceiveth what she hath done, and what remaineth to be done.

She proposeth an *Honest*, *Profitable* and withal, if it may be done, a *Pleasant End*, to her Actions.

Having foreseen the *End*, she looketh out *Means*, as a *Way*, 8. which leadeth to the End; but such as are certain and easie, and fewer rather than more, lest anything should hinder.

She watcheth *Opportunity*, 9. (which having a *bushy fore-head*, 10. and being *bald-pated*, 11. and moreover *having wings*, 12. doth quickly slip away,) and catcheth it.

She goeth on her way warily, for fear she should stumble or go amiss.

ut *Serpens*, 2.
agitque, loquitur, aut cogitat nihil incassum.

Respicit, 3. tanquam in *Speculum*, 4. ad *præterita;* & *prospicit*, 5. tanquam *Telescopio*, 7. *Futura*, seu *Finem*, 6. atque ita perspicit quid egerit, & quid restet agendum.

Actionibus suis præfigit *Scopum*, *Honestum*, *Utilem*, simulque, si fieri potest, *Jucundum*.

Fine prospecto, dispicit *Media*, ceu *Viam*, 8. quæ ducit ad finem, sed certa & facilia; pauciora potiùs quàm plura, ne quid impediat.

Attendit *Occasioni*, 9. (quæ *Fronte Capillata*, 10. sed vertice *calva*, 11. adhæc *alata*, 12. facile elabitur) eamque captat.

In viâ pergit cautè (providè) ne impingat aut aberret.

Diligence. CXI. Sedulitas.

Diligence, 1. loveth labours, avoideth *Sloth*, is always at work, like the *Pismire*, 2. and carrieth together, as she doth, for herself, *Store* of all things, 3.

She doth not always sleep, or make holidays, as the *Sluggard*, 4. and the *Grashopper*, 5. do, whom *Want*, 6. at the last overtaketh.

She pursueth what things she hath undertaken chearfully, even to the end; she putteth nothing off till the morrow, nor doth she sing the *Crow's* song, 7. which saith over and over,

Sedulitas, 1. amat labores, fugit *Ignaviam*, semper est in *opere*, ut *Formica*, 2. & comportat, ut illa, sibi, omnium rerum *Copiam*, 3.

Non semper dormit, ferias agit, aut ut *Ignavus*, 4. & *Cicada*, 5. quos *Inopia*, 6. tandem premit.

Urget incepta alacriter ad finem usque; procrastinat nihil, nec cantat cantilenam *Corvi*, 7. qui ingeminat

Cras, Cras.
After *labours undergone*, and ended, being even wearied, she resteth her self; but being refreshed with *Rest*, that she may not use her self to *Idleness*, she falleth again to her *Business*,
A diligent *Scholar* is like *Bees*, 8. which carry honey from divers *Flowers*, 9. into their *Hive*, 10.

Cras, Cras,
Post *labores exantlatos*, & lassata, quiescit; sed recreata *Quiete*, ne adsuescat *Otio*, redit ad *Negotia*.
Diligens *Discipulus*, similis est *Apibus*, 8. qui congerunt mel ex variis *Floribus*, 9. in *Alveare* suum, 10.

Temperance. CXII. Temperantia.

Temperance, 1. prescribeth a mean to *meat* and *drink*, 2. and restraineth the *desire*, as with a *Bridle*, 3.

Temperantia, 1. præscribit *modum Cibo* & *Potui*, 2. & continet *cupidinem*, ceu *Freno*, 3.

and so moderateth all	& sic moderatur omnia
things, lest any thing too	ne quid
much be done.	nimis fiat.
Revellers	*Heluones* (ganeones)
are made *drunk*, 4.	*inebriantur*, 4.
they *stumble*, 5.	*titubant*, 5.
they *spue*, 6.	*ructant* (vomunt), 6.
and *babble*, 7.	& *rixantur*, 7.
From *Drunkenness*	E *Crapula*
proceedeth *Lasciviousness*;	oritur *Lascivia*;
from this a *lewd Life*	ex hâc *Vita libidinosa*
amongst *Whoremasters*, 8.	inter *Fornicatores*, 8.
and *Whores*, 9.	& *Scorta*, 9.
in *kissing*,	*osculando* (basiando),
touching,	*palpando*,
embracing,	*amplexando*,
and *dancing*, 10.	& *tripudiando*, 10.

Fortitude. CXIII. Fortitudo.

Fortitude, 1.	*Fortitudo*, 1.
is undaunted in adversity,	impavida est in adversis,

and bold as a *Lion*, 2. but not haughty in Prosperity, leaning on her own *Pillar*, 3. *Constancy*, and being the same in all things, ready to undergo both *estates* with an even mind.

She receiveth the strokes of *Misfortune* with the *Shield*, 4. of *Sufferance:* and keepeth off the *Passions*, the enemies of quietness with the *Sword*, 5. of *Valour*.

& confidens ut *Leo*, 2. at non tumida in Secundis, innixa suo *Columini*, 3. *Constantiæ;* & eadem in omnibus, parata ad ferendam utramque *fortunam* æquo animo.

Excipit ictus *Infortunii* *Clypeo*, 4. *Tolerantiæ:* & propellit *Affectus*, hostes Euthymiæ *gladio*, 5. *Virtutis*.

Patience. CXIV. Patientia.

Patience, 1. endureth *Calamities*, 2.

Patientia, 1. tolerat *Calamitates*, 2.

and *Wrongs*, 3. meekly like a *Lamb*, 4. as the Fatherly *chastisement of God*, 5.

In the meanwhile she leaneth upon the *Anchor of Hope*, 6. (as a *Ship*, 7. tossed by waves in the Sea) *she prayeth to God*, 8. weeping, and expecteth the *Sun*, 10. after *cloudy weather*, 9. suffering evils, and hoping better things.

On the contrary, the *impatient person*, 11. waileth, lamenteth, *rageth against himself*, 12. grumbleth like a *Dog*, 13. and yet doth no good; at the last he despaireth, and becometh *his own Murtherer*, 14.

Being full of rage he desireth to revenge wrongs.

& *Injurias*, 3. humiliter ut *Agnus*, 4. tanquam paternam *ferulam Dei*, 5.

Interim innititur *Spei Anchoræ*, 6. (ut *Navis*, 7. fluctuans mari) *Deo supplicat*, 8. illacrymando, & expectat *Phœbum*, 10. post *Nubila*, 9. ferens mala, sperans meliora.

Contra, *Impatiens*, 11. plorat, lamentatur, *debacchatur*, 12. *in seipsum*, obmurmurat ut *Canis*, 13. & tamen nil proficit; tandem desperat, & fit *Autochir*, 14.

Furibundus cupit vindicare injurias.

Humanity. CXV. Humanitas.

Men are made
for one another's *good ;*
therefore let them be *kind.*

Be thou sweet and lovely
in thy *Countenance*, 1.
gentle and civil
in thy *Behaviour* and *Manners*, 2.
affable and true spoken
with thy *Mouth*, 3.
affectionate and *candid*
in thy *Heart*, 4.

So love,
and so shalt thou be loved;
and there will be
a mutual *Friendship*, 5.
as that of *Turtle-doves*, 6.
hearty, gentle, and
wishing well on both parts.

Froward Men are
hateful, teasty, unpleasant.

Homines facti sunt
ad mutua *commoda ;*
ergò sint *humani.*

Sis suavis & amabilis
Vultu, 1.
comis & urbanus
Gestu ac *Moribus*, 2.
affabilis & verax,
Ore, 3.
candens & *candidus*
Corde, 4.

Sic ama,
sic amaberis;
& fiat
mutua *Amicitia*, 5.
ceu *Turturum*, 6.
concors, mansueta,
& benevola utrinque.

Morosi homines, sunt
odiosi, torvi, illepidi.

contentious, *angry*, 7.
cruel, 8.
and implacable,
(rather Wolves and Lions,
than Men)
and such as fall out among
themselves, hereupon
they fight in a *Duel*, 9.
Envy, 10.
wishing ill to others,
pineth away her self.

contentiosi, *iracundi*, 7.
crudeles, 8.
ac implacabiles,
(magis Lupi & Leones,
quàm homines)
& inter se discordes,
hinc
confligunt *Duelle*, 9.
Invidia, 10.
malè cupiendo aliis,
conficit seipsam.

Justice. CXVI. Justitia.

Justice, 1.
is painted, sitting
on a *square stone*, 2. for she
ought to be immoveable;
with *hood-winked eyes*, 3.
that she may not respect
persons;
stopping the left ear, 4.

Justitia, 1.
pingitur, sedens
in *lapide quadrato*, 2. nam
decet esse immobilis;
obvelatis oculis, 3.
ad non respiciendum
personas;
claudens aurem sinistram, 4.

to be reserved	reservandam
for the other party;	alteri parti;
Holding in her right	Tenens dextrâ
Hand a *Sword*, 5.	*Gladium*, 5.
and a *Bridle*, 6.	& *Frænum*, 6.
to punish	ad puniendum
and restrain evil men;	& coërcendum malos;
Besides,	Præterea,
a pair of Balances, 7.	*Stateram*, 7.
in the *right Scale*, 8. where-	cujus *dextræ Lanci*, 8.
of *Deserts*,	*Merita*,
and in the *left*, 9.	*Sinistræ*, 9.
Rewards being put,	*Præmia* imposita,
are made even one with	sibi invicem exequantur,
another, and so good Men	atque ita boni incitantur
are incited to virtue, as it	ad virtutem,
were with *Spurs*, 10.	ceu *Calcaribus*, 10.
In *Bargains*, 11.	In *Contractibus*, 11.
let Men deal candidly,	candidè agatur:
let them stand to their	stetur
Covenants and *Promises;*	*Pactis* & *Promissis;*
let *that which is given one*	*Depositum*,
to keep,	
and *that which is lent*,	& *Mutuum*,
be restored:	reddantur:
let no man be *pillaged*, 12.	nemo *expiletur*, 12.
or *hurt*, 13.	aut *lædatur*, 13.
let every one have his own:	suum cuique tribuatur:
these are the precepts of	hæc sunt præcepta
Justice.	Justitiæ.
Such things as these are	Talio prohibentur,
forbidden in *God's* 5*th.* and	*quinto* & *septimo Dei*
7*th. Cammandment*, and	*Præcepto*, &
deservedly punish'd on the	merito puniuntur
Gallows and the *Wheel*, 14.	*Cruce* ac *Rotâ*, 14.

Liberality. CXVII. Liberalitas.

Liberality, 1.	*Liberalitas*, 1.
keepeth a mean about	servat modum circa
Riches, which she honestly	*Divitias*, quas honestè
seeketh, that she may have	quærit ut habeat
somewhat to bestow on	quod largiatur
them that *want*, 2.	*Egenis*, 2.
She *cloatheth*, 3.	Hos *vestit*, 3.
nourisheth, 4.	*nutrit*, 4.
and *enricheth*, 5.	*ditat*, 5.
these with a *chearful countenance*, 6.	*Vultu hilari*, 6.
and a *winged hand*, 7.	& *Manu alatâ*, 7.
She submitteth her	Subjicit
wealth, 8. to her self, not	*opes*, 8. sibi, non
her self to it, as the *covetous man*, 9. doth, who hath,	se illis, ut *Avarus*, 9. qui habet,
that he may have, and is	ut habeat, &
not the *Owner*,	non est *Possessor*
but the *Keeper* of his goods,	sed *Custos* bonorum suorum,
and being unsatiable,	& insatiabilis,
always *scrapeth together*, 10.	semper *corradit*, 10.
with his Nails.	Unguibus suis.

Moreover he spareth and keepeth, *hoarding up*, 11. that he may always have.	Sed & parcit & adservat, *occludendo*, 11. ut semper habeat.
But the *Prodigal*, 12. badly spendeth things well gotten, and at the last wanteth.	At *Prodigus*, 12. malè disperdit benè parta, ac tandem eget.

CXVIII.
Society betwixt Man and Wife.

Societas Conjugalis.

Marriage was appointed by God in Paradise, for mutual *help*, and the *Propagation* of mankind.	*Matrimonium* institutum est à Deo in Paradiso, ad mutuum *adjutorium*, & *propagationem* generis humani.
A young man (*a single man*) being to be married, should be furnished either with *Wealth*, or a *Trade* and *Science*,	*Vir Juvenis* (*Cælebs*) conjugium initurus, instructus sit aut *Opibus*, aut *Arte* & *Scientiâ*,

which may serve for getting a living; that he may be able to maintain a *Family*.	quæ sit de pane lucrando; ut possit sustentare *Familiam*.
Then he chooseth himself a *Maid* that is *Marriageable*, (or a *Widow*) whom he loveth; nevertheless a greater Regard is to be had of *Virtue*, and *Honesty*, than of *Beauty* or *Portion*.	Deinde eligit sibi *Virginem Nubilem*, (aut *Viduam*) quam adamat; ubi tamen major ratio habenda *Virtutis* & *Honestatis*, quàm *Formæ* aut *Dotis*.
Afterwards, he doth not betroth her to himself closely, but entreateth for her as a *Woer*, first to the *Father*, 1. and then the *Mother*, 2. or the *Guardians*, or *Kinsfolks*, by such *as help to make the match*, 3.	Posthæc, non clam despondet sibi eam, sed ambit, ut *Procus*, apud *Patrem*, 1. & *Matrem*, 2. vel apud *Tutores*, & *Cognatos*, per *Pronubos*, 3.
When she is espous'd to him, he becometh the *Bridegroom*, 4. and she the *Bride*, 5. and the *Contract* is made. and an *Instrument* of *Dowry*, 6. is written.	Eâ sibi desponsâ, fit *Sponsus*, 4. & ipsa *Sponsa*, 5. fiuntque *Sponsalia*, & scribitur *Instrumentum Dotale*, 6.
At the last the *Wedding* is made, where they are joined together by the *Priest*, 7. giving their *Hands*, 8. one to another. and *Wedding-rings*, 9. then they feast with the witnesses that are invited.	Tandem fiunt *Nuptiæ* ubi copulantur à *Sacerdote*, 7. datis *Manibus*, 8. ultrò citroque, & *Annulis Nuptialibus*, 9. tum epulantur cum invitatis testibus.
After this they are called *Husband* and *Wife;* when she is dead he becometh a *Widower*.	Abhinc dicuntur *Maritus* & *Uxor;* hâc mortuâ ille fit *Viduus*.

CXIX.

The Tree of Consanguinity,

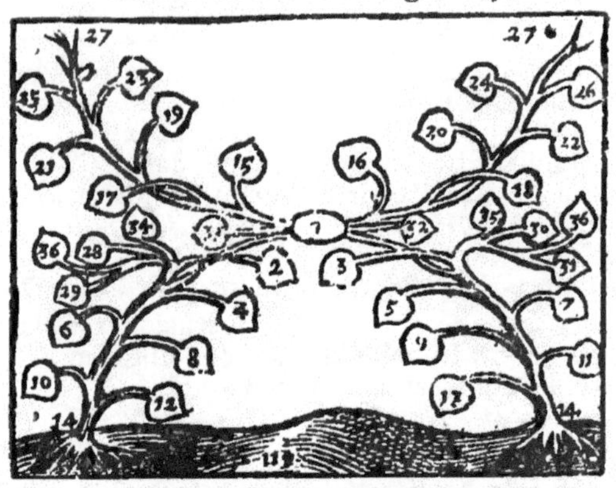

Arbor Consanguinitatis.

In *Consanguinity*
there touch a *Man*, 1.
in *Lineal Ascent*,
the *Father*
(the *Father-in-law*), 2.
and the *Mother*
(the *Mother-in-law*), 3.
the *Grandfather*, 4.
and the *Grandmother*, 5.
the *Great Grandfather*, 6.
and the *Great Grandmother*,
7. the *great great*
Grandfather, 8.
the *great great*
Grandmother, 9.
the *great great Grand-*
father's Father, 10.
the *great great Grand-*
mother's Mother, 11.

Hominem, 1.
Consanguinitate attingunt,
in Linea ascendenti,
Pater
(*Vitricus*), 2.
& *Mater*
(*Noverca*), 3.
Avus, 4.
& *Avia*, 5.
Proavus, 6.
& *Proavia*, 7.
Abavus, 8.
& *Abavia*, 9.
Atavus, 10.
& *Atavia*, 11

the *great great Grandfather's Grandfather*, 12.	*Tritavus*, 12.
the *great great Grandmother's Grandmother*, 13.	& *Tritavia*, 13.
Those beyond these are called *Ancestors*, 14. . . 14.	Ulteriores dicuntur *Majores*, 14. . . 14.
In a *Lineal descent*,	In *Linea descendenti*,
the *Son* (*the son-in-law*), 15.	*Filius* (*Privignus*), 15.
and the *Daughter*, (*the Daughter-in-law*), 16.	& *Filia* (*Privigna*), 16.
the *Nephew*, 17.	*Nepos*, 17.
and the *Neece*, 18.	& *Neptis*, 18.
the *Nephews Son*, 19. and	*Pronepos*, 19.
the *Nephews Daughter*, 20.	& *Proneptis*, 26.
the *Nephews Nephew*, 21.	*Abnepos*, 21.
and the *Neeces Neece*, 22.	& *Abneptis*, 22.
the *Nephews Nephews Son*, 23.	*Atnepos*, 23.
the *Neeces Neeces Daughter*, 24.	& *Atneptis*, 24.
the *Nephews Nephews Nephew*, 25.	*Trinepos*, 25.
	& *Trineptis*, 26.
the *Neeces Neeces Neece*, 26.	Ulteriores dicuntur
Those beyond these are called *Posterity*, 27. . . 27.	*Posteri*, 27. . . . 27.
In a *Collateral Line* are	In *Linea Collaterali*
the *Uncle by the Fathers side*, 28.	sunt *Patruus*, 28.
and the *Aunt by the Fathers side*, 29.	& *Amita*, 29.
the *Uncle by the Mothers side*, 30.	*Avunculus*, 30.
and the *Aunt by the Mothers side*, 31.	& *Matertera*, 31.
the *Brother*, 32.	*Frater*, 32.
and the *Sister*, 33.	& *Soror*, 33.
the *Brothers Son*, 34.	*Patruelis*, 34.
the *Sisters Son*, 35.	*Sobrinus*, 35.
and the *Cousin by the Brother* and *Sister*, 36.	& *Amitinus*, 36.

CXX.

The Society betwixt Parents and Children.

Societas Parentalis.

Married Persons, (by the blessing of God) have *Issue,* and become *Parents.*

The *Father,* 1. begetteth and the *Mother,* 2. beareth *Sons,* 3. and *Daughters,* 4. (sometimes *Twins*).

The *Infant,* 5. is wrapped in *Swadling-cloathes,* 6. is laid in a *Cradle,* 7. is suckled by the Mother with her *Breasts,* 8. and fed with *Pap,* 9.

Afterwards it learneth to go by a *Standing-stool,* 10.

Conjuges, (ex benedictione Dei) suscipiunt *Sobolem* (Prolem) & fiunt *Parentes.*

Pater, 1. generat & *Mater,* 2. parit *Filios,* 3. & *Filias,* 4. (aliquando *Gemellos*).

Infans, 5. involvitur *Fasciis,* 6. reponitur in *Cunas,* 7. lactatur a matre *Uberibus,* 8. & nutritur *Pappis,* 9.

Deinde discit incedere *Seperasto,* 10.

playeth with *Rattles*, 11. and beginneth to speak.

As it beginneth to grow older, it is accustomed to *Piety*, 12. and *Labour*, 13. and is chastised, 14. if it be not dutiful.

Children owe to Parents Reverence and Service.

The Father maintaineth his Children *by taking pains*, 15.

ludit *Crepundiis*, 11. & incipit fari.

Crescente ætate, adsuescit *Pietati*, 12. & *Labori*, 13. & castigatur, 14. si non sit morigerus.

Liberi debent Parentibus Cultum & Officium.

Pater sustentat Liberos, *laborando*, 15.

CXXI.

The Society betwixt Masters and Servants.

Societas herilis.

The *Master* (*the goodman of the House*), 1. hath *Men-servants*, 2.

Herus (*Pater familias*), 1. habet *Famulos* (*Servos*), 2.

the *Mistress* (*the good wife of the House*), 3. *Maidens*, 4.	*Hera* (*Mater familias*), 3. *Ancillas*, 4.
They appoint these their *Work*, 6. and divide *them their tasks*, 5. which are faithfully to be done by them without murmuring and loss: for which their *Wages*, and *Meat* and *Drink* is allowed them.	Illi mandant his *Opera*, 6. & distribuunt *Laborum Pensa*, 5. qua ab his fideliter sunt exsequenda sine murmure & dispendio; pro quo *Merces* & *Alimonia* præbentur ipsis.
A *Servant* was heretofore a *Slave*, over whom the Master had power of life and death.	*Servus* olim erat *Mancipium*, in quem Domino potestas fuit vitæ & necis
At this day the poorer sort serve in a free manner, being hired for Wages.	Hodiè pauperiores serviunt liberè, conducti mercede.

A City. CXXII. Urbs.

Of many Houses is made a *Village*, 1.	Ex multis Domibus fit *Pagus*, 1.

or a *Town*, or a *City*, 2.
That and this are fenced and begirt with a *Wall*, 3.
a *Trench*, 4.
Bulwarks, 5.
and *Pallisadoes*, 6.
Within the Walls is the *void Place*, 7.
without, the *Ditch*, 8.
In the Walls are *Fortresses*, 9.
and *Towers*, 10.
Watch-Towers, 11. are upon the higher places.
The entrance into a City is made out of the *Suburbs*, 12. through *Gates*, 13.
over the *Bridge*, 14.
The *Gate* hath a *Portcullis*, 15.
a *Draw-bridge*, 16.
two-leaved Doors, 17.
Locks and *Bolts*,
as also *Barrs*, 18.
In the Suburbs are *Gardens*, 19.
and *Garden-houses*, 20. and also *Burying-places*, 21.

vel *Oppidum*, vel *Urbs*, 2.
Istud & hæc muniuntur & cinguntur *Mœnibus* (*Muro*), 3. *Vallo*, 4.
Aggeribus, 5.
& *Vallis*, 6.
Intra muros est *Pomœrium*, 7.
extrà, *Fossa*, 8.
In mœnibus sunt *Propugnacula*, 9.
& *Turres*, 10.
Specula, 11. extant in editioribus locis.
Ingressus in Urbem fit ex *Suburbio*, 12.
per *Portam*, 13.
super *Pontem*, 14.
Porta habet *Cataractas*, 15.
Pontem versatilem, 16.
Valvas, 17.
Claustra & *Repagula*,
ut & *Vectes*, 18.
In Suburbiis sunt *Horti*, 19.
& *Suburbana*, 20.
ut & *Cœmeteria*, 21.

CXXIII.
The inward parts of a City.

Interiora Urbis.

Within the City are	Intra urbem sunt
Streets, 1.	*Plateæ* (Vici), 1.
paved with Stones;	stratæ Lapidibus;
Market-places, 2.	*Fora*, 2.
(in some places with	(alicubi cum
Galleries), 3.	*Porticibus*), 3.
and *narrow Lanes*, 4.	& *Angiportus*, 4.
The Publick Buildings	Publica ædificia
are in the middle of the	sunt in medio Urbis,
City, the *Church*, 5.	*Templum*, 5.
the *School*, 6.	*Schola*, 6.
the *Guild-Hall*, 7.	*Curia*, 7.
the *Exchange*, 8.	*Domus Mercaturæ*, 8.
About the Walls and the	Circa Mœnia, & Portas
Gates are the *Magazine*, 9.	*Armamentarium*, 9.
the *Granary*, 10.	*Granarium*, 10.
Inns, *Ale-houses*,	*Diversoria*, *Popinæ*,
Cooks-shops, 11.	& *Cauponæ*, 11.

the *Play-house*, 12.	*Theatrum*, 12.
and the *Spittle*, 13.	*Nosodochium*, 13.
In the by-places	In recessibus,
are *Houses of Office*, 14.	*Foricæ* (Cloacæ), 14.
and the *Prison*, 15.	& *Custodia* (Carcer), 15.
In the chief Steeple	In turre primariâ
is the *Clock*, 16. and the *Watchmans* Dwelling, 17.	est *Horologium*, 16. & habitatio *Vigilum*, 17.
In the Streets are *Wells*, 18.	In Plateis sunt *Putei*, 18.
The *River*, 19. or *Beck*, runneth about the City, serveth to wash away the *filth*.	*Fluvius*, 19. vel *Rivus*, interfluens Urbem, inservit eluendis *sordibus*.
The *Tower*, 20. standeth in the highest part of the City.	*Arx*, 20. extat in summo Urbis.

Judgment. CXXIV. Judicium.

The best Law, is	Optimum Jus, est
a quiet *agreement*,	placida *conventio*,
made either by themselves,	facta vel ab ipsis,

betwixt whom the sute is,
or by an *Umpire*.

If this do not proceed,
they come into *Court*, 1.
(heretofore they judg'd
in the Market-place; at
this day in the *Moot-hall*)
in which the *Judge*, 2.
sitteth with his *Assessors*, 3.
the *Clerk*, 4. taketh
their Votes in writing.

The *Plaintiff*, 5.
accuseth the *Defendant*, 6.
and produceth *Witnesses*, 7.
against him.

The *Defendant* excuseth
himself by a *Counsellor*, 8.
whom the Plaintiff's *Counsellor*, 9. contradicts.

Then the *Judge*
pronounceth *Sentence*,
acquitting the *innocent*,
and condemning
him that is *guilty*,
to a *Punishment*,
or a *Fine*,
or *Torment*.

inter quos lis est
vel ab *Arbitro*.

Hæc si non procedit,
venitur in *Forum*, 1.
(olim judicabant
in Foro,
hodiè in *Prætorio*)
cui *Judex* (Prætor), 2.
præsidet cum *Assessoribus*,
3. *Dicographus*, 4. excipit
Vota calamo.

Actor, 5.
accusat *Reum*, 6.
& producit *Testes*, 7.
contra illum.

Reus excusat
se per *Advocatum*, 8.
cui Actoris *Procurator*, 9.
contradicit.

Tum *Judex*
Sententiam pronunciat,
absolvens *insontem*,
& damnans
sontem
ad *Pœnam*,
vel *Mulctam*,
vel ad *Supplicium*.

CXXV.
The Tormenting of Malefactors.

Supplicia Malefactorum.

Malefactors, 1.	*Malefici*, 1.
are brought	producuntur,
from the *Prison*, 3.	è *Carcere*, 3.
(where they are wont to be	(ubi torqueri solent)
tortured) by *Serjeants*, 2.	per *Lictores*, 2.
or *dragg'd with a Horse*, 15.	vel *Equo raptantur*, 15.
to place of *Execution.*	ad locum *Supplicii.*
Thieves, 4.	*Fures*, 4.
are hanged by the *Hang-*	suspenduntur a *Carnifice*,6.
man, 6. on a *Gallows*, 5.	in *Patibulo*, 5.
Whoremasters	*Mœchi*
are beheaded, 7.	decollantur, 7.
Murtherers	*Homicidæ* (Sicarii)
and *Robbers* are	ac *Latrones* (Piratæ)
either laid upon a *Wheel*, 8.	vel imponuntur *Rotæ*
having their *Legs broken*,	*crucifragio plexi*, 8.
or fastened upon a *Stake*, 9.	vel *Palo* infiguntur, 9.
Witches	*Striges* (Lamiæ)

are burnt in a *great Fire*, 10.	cremantur super *Rogum*, 10.
Some before they are executed have their *Tongues cut out*, 11.	Quidam antequam supplicio afficiantur *elinguantur*, 11.
or have their *Hand*, 12.	aut plectuntur *Manu*, 12.
cut off upon a *Block*, 13. or	super *Cippum*, 13.
are burnt with *Pincers*, 14.	aut *Forcipibus*, 14. uruntur
They that have their Life given them,	Vitâ donati,
are set on the *Pillory*, 16.	constringuntur *Numellis*, 16.
or *strapado'd*, 17. are	luxantur, 17.
set upon a *wooden Horse*, 18.	imponuntur *Equuleo*, 18.
have their *Ears cut off*, 19.	*truncantur Auribus*, 19.
are *whipped with Rods*, 20.	*cæduntur Virgis*, 20.
are branded,	Stigmate notantur,
are banished,	relegantur,
are condemned to the *Gallies*, or to perpetual Imprisonment.	damnantur ad *Triremes*, vel ad Carcerem perpetuum.
Traytors are pull'd in pieces with four *Horses*.	*Perduelles* discerpuntur *Quadrigis*.

Merchandizing. CXXVI. Mercatura.

Wares
brought from other places
are either exchanged
in an *Exchange*, 1
or exposed to sale
in *Warehouses*, 2.
and they are sold
for *Money*, 3.
being either measured
with an *Eln*, 4.
or weighed
in a *pair of Balances*, 5.

Shop-keepers, 6.
Pedlars, 7.
and *Brokers*, 8.
would also be called
Merchants, 9.

The *Seller*
braggeth of a thing
that is to be sold,

Merces,
aliunde allatæ, aliunde
vel commutantur
in *Domo Commerciorum*, 1,
vel exponuntur venum
in *Tabernis Mercimoniorum*,
2. & venduntur
pro *Pecuniâ* (monetâ), 3.
vel mensuratæ
Ulnâ, 4.
vel ponderatæ
Librâ, 5.

Tabernarii. 6.
Circumforanei, 7.
& *Scrutarii*, 8.
etiam volunt dici
Mercatores, 9.

Venditor
ostentat rem
promercalem,

and setteth the rate of it,	& indicat pretium,
and how much	quanti
it may be sold for.	liceat.
The *Buyer*, 10. cheapneth	*Emptor*, 10. licetur,
and offereth the price.	& pretium offert.
If any one	Si quis
bid *against him*, 11. the	*contralicetur*, 11.
thing is delivered to him	ei res addicitur
that promiseth the most.	qui pollicetur plurimum.

CXXVII.

Measures and Weights. / Mensuræ & Pondera.

We measure things that	Res continuas metimur
hang together with an *Eln*,	*Ulnâ*, 1.
1. liquid things	liquidas
with a *Gallon*, 2.	*Congio*, 2.
and dry things	aridas
by a *two-bushel Measure*, 3.	*Medimno*, 3.
We try the heaviness of	Gravitatem rerum ex-
things by *Weights*, 4.	perimur *Ponderibus*, 4.
and *Balances*, 5.	& *Librâ* (bilance), 5.
In this is first	In hâc primò est

the *Beam*, 6.
in the midst whereof is a
little *Axle-tree*, 7. above
the *cheeks* and the *hole*, 8.
in which the *Needle*, 9.
moveth it self to and fro:
on both sides
are the *Scales*, 10.
hanging by *little Cords*, 11.
The *Brasiers balance*, 12.
weigheth things by hanging them on a *Hook*, 13.
and the *Weight*, 14.
opposite to them which
in (a) weigheth just as
much as the thing,
in (b) twice so much
in (c) thrice so much, &c.

Jugum (Scapus), 6.
in cujus medio
Axiculus, 7. superiùs
trutina & *agina*, 8.
in quâ *Examen*, 9.
sese agitat:
utrinque
sunt *Lances*, 10.
pendentes *Funiculis*, 11.
Statera, 12.
ponderat res, suspendendo
illas *Unco*, 13.
& *Pondus*, 14.
ex opposito, quod
in (a) æquiponderat
rei,
in (b) his tantum,
in (c) ter, &c.

Physick. CXXVIII. Ars Medica.

The *Patient*, 1.
sendeth for a *Physician*, 2.

Ægrotans, 1.
accersit *Medicum*, 2.

who feeleth his *Pulse*, 3, and looketh upon his *Water*, 4. and then prescribeth a *Receipt* in a *Bill*, 5.

That is made ready by an *Apothecary*, 6. in a *Apothecaries Shop*, 7. where *Drugs* are kept in *Drawers*, 8. *Boxes*, 9. and *Gally-pots*, 10.

And it is either a *Potion*, 11. or *Powder*, 12. or *Pills*, 13. or *Trochisks*, 14. or an *Electuary*, 15.

Diet and *Prayer*, 16. is the best *Physick*.

The *Chirurgeon*, 18. cureth *Wounds*, 17. and *Ulcers*, with *Plasters*, 19.

qui tangit ipsius *Arteriam*, 3. & inspicit *Urinam*, 4. tum præscribit *Medicamentum* in *Schedula*, 5.

Istud paratur à *Pharmacopœo*, 6. in *Pharmacopolio*, 7. ubi *Pharmaca* adservantur in *Capsulis*, 8. *Pyxidibus*, 9. & *Lagenis*, 10.

Estque vel *Potio*, 11. vel *Pulvis*, 12. vel *Pillulæ*, 13. vel *Pastilli*, 14. vel *Electuarium*, 15.

Diæta & *Oratio*, 16. est optima *Medicina*.

Chirurgus, 18. curat *Vulnera*, 17. & *Ulcera*, *Spleniis* (emplastris), 19.

A Burial. CXXIX. Sepultura.

Dead Folks
heretofore were burned,
and their Ashes
put into an *Urn*, 1.
We enclose
our *dead Folks*
in a *Coffin*, 2.
lay them upon a *Bier*, 3.
and see they be carried out
in a *Funeral Pomp*
towards the *Church-yard*, 4.
where they are laid
in a *Grave*, 6.
by the *Bearers*, 5.
and are interred;
this is covered with
a *Grave-stone*, 7.
and is adorned
with *Tombs*, 8.
and *Epitaphs*, 9.

Defuncti
olim cremabantur,
& Cineres
recondebantur in *Urna*, 1.
Nos includimus
nostros *Demortuos*
Loculo, (*Capulo*), 2.
imponimus *Feretro*, 3.
& curamus efferri
Pompâ Funebri
versus *Cœmeterium*, 4.
ubi inferuntur,
Sepulchro, 6.
a *Vespillonibus*, 5.
& humantur;
hoc tegitur
Cippo, 7.
& ornatur
Monumentis, 8.
ac *Epitaphiis*, 9.

As the Corps go along *Psalms* are sung, and the *Bells* are rung, 10.	Funere prodeunte, *Hymni* cantantur, & *Campanæ*, 10. pulsantur.

A Stage-play. CXXX. Ludus Scenicus.

In a *Play-house*, 1. (which is trimmed with *Hangings*, 2. and covered with *Curtains*, 3.) *Comedies* and *Tragedies* are acted, wherein memorable things are represented; as here, the History of the *Prodigal Son*, 4. and his *Father*, 5. by whom he is entertain'd, being return'd home.	In *Theatro*, 1. (quod vestitur *Tapetibus*, 2. & tegitur *Sipariis*, 3.) *Comediæ* vel *Tragœdiæ* aguntur, quibus repræsentantur res memorabiles ut hic, Historia de *Filio Prodigo*, 4. & *Patre*, 5. ipsius, à quo recipitur, domum redux.
The *Players* act being in disguise; the *Fool*, 6. maketh Jests.	*Actores* (*Histriones*) agunt personati; *Morio*, 6. dat Jocos.

The chief of the Specta-	Spectatorum primarii,
tors sit in the *Gallery*, 7.	sedent in *Orchestra*, 7.
the common sort stand	plebs stat
on the *Ground*, 8.	in *Cavea*, 8.
and clap the hands,	& plaudit,
if anything please them.	si quid arridet.

Sleights. CXXXI. Præstigiæ.

The *Tumbler*, 1.	*Præstigiator*, 1.
maketh several *Shows*	facit varia *Spectacula*,
by the nimbleness of his	volubilitate
body, walking to and fro	corporis, deambulando
on his hands,	*manibus*,
leaping	saliendo
through a *Hoop*, 2. &c.	per *Circulum*, 2. &c.
Sometimes also	Interdum etiam
he *danceth*, 4.	*tripudiat*, 4.
having on a Vizzard.	Larvatus.
The *Jugler*, 3.	*Agyrta*, 3.
sheweth *sleights*,	facit *præstigias*
out of a *Purse*.	è *Marsupio*.

The *Rope-dancer*, 5.	*Funambulus*, 5.
goeth and danceth	graditur & saltat
upon a *Rope*,	super *Funem*,
holdeth a *Poise*, 6.	tenens *Halterem*, 6.
in his hand;	manu;
or hangeth himself	aut suspendit se
by the *hand* or *foot*, 7. &c.	*manu* vel *pede*, 7. &c.

The Fencing-School. CXXXII. Palestra.

Fencers	*Pugiles*
meet in a Duel	congrediuntur Duello
in a *Fencing-place*,	in *Palestra*,
fighting with *Swords*, 1.	decertantes vel *Gladiis*, 1.
or *Pikes*, 2.	vel *Hastilibus*, 2.
and *Halberds*, 3.	& *Bipennibus*, 3.
or *Short-swords*, 4.	vel *Semispathis*, 4.
or *Rapiers*, 5.	vel *Ensibus*, 5.
having balls at the point	*mucronem obligatis*,
(lest they wound one	(ne lædet
another mortally)	lethaliter)
or with *two edged-Swords*	vel *Frameis*
and a *Dagger*, 6. together.	& *Pugione*, 6. simul.

Wrestlers, 7. (among the Romans in time past were nayked and anointed with Oyl) take hold of one another and strive whether can throw the other, especially by *tripping up his heels*, 8.

Luctatores, 7. (apud Romanos olim nudi & inuncti Oleo) prehendunt se invicem & annituntur uter alterum prosternere possit, præprimis *supplantando*, 8.

Hood-winked Fencers, 9. fought with their fists in a ridiculous strife, to wit, with their Eyes coverered.

Andabatæ, 9. pugnabant pugnis ridiculo certamine, nimirum Oculis obvelatis.

Tennis-play. CXXXIII. Ludus Pilæ.

In a *Tennis Court*, 1. they play with a *Ball*, 2. which one throweth, and another taketh, and sendeth it back with a *Racket*, 3.

In *Sphæristerio*, 1. luditur *Pilâ*, 2. quam alter mittit, alter excipit, & remittit *Reticulo*, 3.

and that is the Sport
of Noble Men
to stir their Body.
A *Wind-ball*, 4.
being filled with Air,
by means of a *Ventil*,
is tossed to and fro
with the *Fist*, 5.
in the open Air.

idque est Lusus
Nobilium ad
commotionem Corporis.
Follis (pila magna), 4.
distenta Aere
ope *Epistomii*,
reverberberatur
Pugno, 5.
sub Dio.

Dice-play. CXXXIV. Ludus Aleæ.

We play with *Dice*, 1.
either they that throw the most *take up all*;
or we throw them
through a *Casting-box*, 2.
upon a *Board*, 3.
marked with figures,
and this is *Dice-players game*
at *casting Lots*.
Men play by *Luck* and *Skill* at *Tables*.
in a *pair of Tables*, 4.

Tesseris (*talis*), 1. ludimus vel *Plistobolindam*;
vel immittimus illas
per *Frittillum*, 2.
in *Tabellam*, 3.
notatam numeris,
idque est *Ludas Sortilegii*
Aleatorum.
Sorte & *Arte* luditur
Calculis
in *Alveo aleatorio*, 4.

and at *Cards*, 5.
We play at *Chesse* on a *Chesse-board*, 6. where only art beareth the sway.
The most ingenious Game is the Game of *Chesse*, 7. wherein as it were two Armies fight together in Battel.

& *Chartis lusoriis*, 5.
Ludimus *Abaculis* in *Abaco*, 6. ubi sola ars regnat.
Ingeniosissimus Ludus est Ludus *Latrunculorum*, 7. quo veluti duo Exercitus confligunt Prælio.

Races. CXXXV. Cursus Certamina.

Boys exercise themselves by running, either upon the *Ice*, 1. in *Scrick-shoes*, 2. where they are carried also upon *Sleds*, 3. or in the open Field, making a *Line*, 4. which he that desireth to win, ought to touch, but not to run beyond it.
Heretofore *Runners*, 5. run betwixt *Rails*, 6.

Pueri exercent se cursu, sive super *Glaciem*, 1. *Diabatris*, 2. ubi etiam vehuntur *Trahis*, 3. sive in Campo, designantes *Lineam*, 4. quam qui vincere cupit debet attingere, at non ultrâ procurrere.
Olim decurrebant *Cursores*, 5. inter *Cancellos*, 6.

to the *Goal*, 7. and	ad *Metam*, 7. &
he that toucheth it first	qui primum contingebat
receiveth the *Prize*, 8. from	eam, accipiebat *Brabeum*,
him that gave the prize, 9.	(*præmium*), 8. à *Brabeuta*, 9.
At this day *Tilting*	Hodie *Hastiludia*
(or the quintain) is used,	habentur,
(where a *Hoop*, 11.	(ubi *Circulus*, 11.
is struck at with	petitur
a *Truncheon*, 10.) in-	*Lancea*, 10.)
stead of *Horse-races*, which	loco *Equiriorum*, quæ
are grown out of use.	abierunt in desuetudinem.

Boys Sport. CXXXVI. Ludi Pueriles.

Boys use to play	*Pueri* solent ludere
either with *Bowling-stones*	vel *Globis fictilibus*, 1.
1. or throwing a *Bowl*, 2.	vel jactantes *Globum*, 2.
at *Nine-pins*, 3.	ad *Conas*, 3.
or striking a *Ball*,	vel mittentes *Sphærulam*
through a *Ring*, 5.	per *Annulum*, 5.
with a *Bandy*, 4.	*Clava*, 4.
or scourging a *Top*, 6.	versantes *Turbinem*, 6.
with a *Whip*, 7.	*Flagello*, 7.

or shooting with a *Trunk*, 8. and a *Bow*, 9. or going upon *Stilts*, 10. or tossing and swinging themselves upon a *Merry-totter*, 11.

vel jaculantes *Sclopo*, 8. & *Arcu*, 9. vel incidentes *Grallis*, 10. vel super *Petaurum*, 11. se agitantes & oscillantes.

CXXXVII.

The Kingdom and the Region.

Regnum & Regio.

Many *Cities* and *Villages* make a *Region* and a *Kingdom*.

The *King* or *Prince* resideth in the *chief City*, 1. the *Noblemen*, *Lords*, and *Earls* dwell in the *Castles*, 2. that lie about it; the *Country People* dwell in *Villages*, 3.

Multæ *Urbes* & *Pagi* faciunt *Regionem* & *Regnum*.

Rex aut *Princeps* sedet in *Metropoli*. 1. *Nobiles*, *Barones*, & *Comites* habitant in *Arcibus*, 2. circumjacentibus; *Rustici* in *Pagis*, 3.

He hath his *toll-places*	Habet *telonia sua*
upon *navigable Rivers*, 4.	juxta *Flumina navigabilia*,
and *high-Roads*, 5.	4. & *Vias regias*, 5.
where *Portage* and *Tollage*	ubi *Portorum* & *Vectigal*
is exacted of them	exigitur
that sail	a navigantibus
or travel.	& iter facientibus.

CXXXVIII.

Regal Majesty. Regia Majestas.

The *King*, 1.	*Rex*, 1.
sitteth on his *Throne*, 2.	sedet in suo *Solio*, 2.
in Kingly State,	in regio splendore,
with a stately *Habit*, 3.	magnifico *Habitu*, 3.
crowned with a *Diadem*, 4.	redimitus *Diademate*, 4.
holding a *Scepter*, 5.	tenens *Sceptrum*, 5.
in his Hand,	manu,
being attended with	stipatus
a Company of *Courtiers*.	frequentiâ *Aulicorum*.
The chief among these,	Inter hos primarii sunt
are the *Chancellor*, 6.	*Cancellarius*, 6.
with the *Counsellors*	cum *Consiliariis*

and *Secretaries*,	& *Secretariis*,
the *Lord-marshall*, 7.	*Præfectus Prætorii*, 7.
the *Comptroller*, 8.	*Aulæ Magister*, 8.
the *Cup-bearer*, 9.	*Pocillator* (pincerna), 9.
the *Taster*, 10.	*Dapifer*, 10.
the *Treasurer*, 11.	*Thesaurarius*, 11.
the *High Chamberlain*, 12.	*Archi-Cubicularius*, 12.
and the *Master of the Horse*, 13.	& *Stabuli Magister*, 13.
There are subordinate to these	Subordinantur his
the *Noble Courtiers*, 14.	*Nobiles Aulici*, 14.
the *Noble Pages*, 15.	*Nobile Famulitium*, 15.
with the *Chamberlains*,	cum *Cubiculariis*,
and *Lacquies*, 16.	& *Cursoribus*, 16.
the *Guard*, 17.	*Stipatores*, 17.
with their *Attendance*.	cum *Satellitio*.
He solemnly giveth Audience to the *Ambassadors* of Foreign Princes, 18.	Solemniter recipit *Legatos* exterorum, 18.
He sendeth his *Vice-gerents*, *Deputies*, *Governors*, *Treasurers*, and *Ambassadors* to other places,	Ablegat *Vicarios* suos, *Administratores*, *Præfectos*, *Quæstores*, & *Legatos*, aliorsum,
to whom he sendeth *new Commissions* ever and anon by the *Posts*, 19.	quibus mittit *Mandata nova* subinde per *Veredarios*, 19.
The *Fool*, 20.	*Morio*, 20.
maketh Laughter by his toysom Actions.	movet Risum ludicris Actionibus.

The Soldier. CXXXIX. Miles.

If we be to make War *Soldiers* are lifted, 1.

Their *Arms* are a *Head-piece*, 2. (which is adorned with a *Crest*) and the *Armour*, whose parts are a *Collar*, 3. a *Breast-plate*, 4. *Arm-pieces*, 5. *Leg-pieces*, 6. *Greaves*, 7. with a *Coat of Mail*, 8. and a *Buckler*, 9. these are the defensive Arms.

The offensive are a *Sword*, 10. a *two-edged Sword*, 11. a *Falchion*, 12. which are put up into a *Scabbard*, 13. and are girded with a *Girdle*, 14. or *Belt*, 15.

Si bellandum est scribuntur *Milites*. 1.

Horum *Arma* sunt, *Galea* (Cassis, 2.) (quæ ornatur *Cristâ*) & *Armatura*, cujus partes *Torquis ferreus*, 3. *Thorax*, 4. *Brachialia*, 5. *Ocreæ ferreæ*, 6. *Manicæ*, 7. cum *Lorica*, 8. & *Scuto* (Clypeo), 9. hæc sunt Arma defensiva.

Offensiva sunt *Gladius*, 10. *Framea*, 11. & *Acinaces*, 12. qui reconduntur *Vaginâ*, 13. accinguntur *Cingulo*, 14. vel *Baltheo*, 15.

(a *Scarf*, 16.
serveth for ornament)
a *two handed-Sword*, 17.
and a *Dagger*, 18.
In these is the *Haft*, 19.
with the *Pummel*, 20.
and the *Blade*, 21.
having a *Point*, 22.
in the middle are the
Back, 23. and the *Edge*, 24.
The other Weapons are
a *Pike*, 25. a *Halbert*, 26.
(in which is the *Haft*, 27.
and the *Head*, 28.) a
Club, 29. and a *Whirlebat*, 30.
They fight at a distance
with *Muskets*, 31.
and *Pistols*, 32. which
are charged with *Bullets*,
33. out of a *Bullet-bag*, 34.
and with *Gun-powder*
out of a *Bandalier*, 35.

(*Fascia militaris*, 16.
inservit ornatui)
Romphæa, 17.
& *Pugio*, 18.
In his est *Manubrium*, 19.
cum *Pomo*, 20.
& *Verutum*, 21.
Cuspidatum, 22.
in medio
Dorsum, 23. & *Acies*, 24.
Reliqua arma sunt
Hasta, 25. *Bipennis*, 26.
(in quibus *Hastile*, 27.
& *Mucro*, 28.)
Clava, 29. & *Cæstus*, 30.
Pugnatur eminùs
Bombardis (Sclopetis), 31.
& *Sclopis*, 32. quæ
onerantur *Globis*, 33.
è *Theca bombardica*, 34.
& *Pulvere nitrato*
è *Pyxide pulveraria*, 35.

The Camps. CXL. Castra.

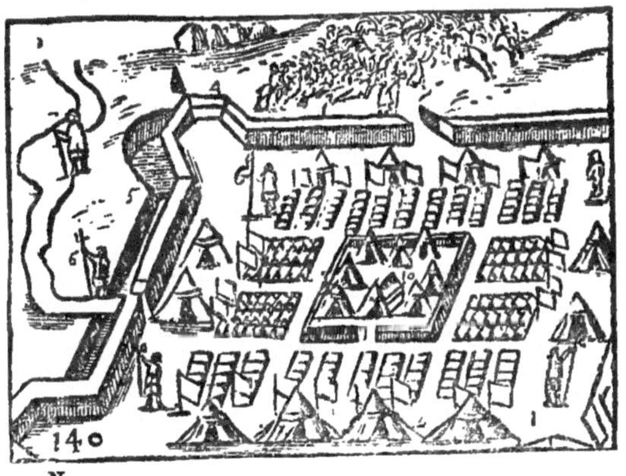

When a *Design* is undertaken the *Camp*, 1. is pitched and the *Tents* of *Canvas*, 2. or *Straw*, 3. are fastned with *Stakes ;* and they entrench them about for security's sake, with *Bulwarks*, 4. and *Ditches*, 5. *Sentinels*, 6. are also set; and *Scouts*, 7. are sent out.

Sallyings out, 8. are made for Forage and Plunder-sake, where they often cope with the *Enemy*, 9 in skirmishing.

The *Pavilion* of the *Lord General* is in the midst of the *Camp*, 10.

Expeditione susceptâ, *Castra*, 1. locantur & *Tentoria Linteis*, 2. vel *Stramentis*, 3. figuntur *Paxillis ;* eaque circumdant, securitatis gratiâ *Aggeribus*, 4. & *Fossis*, 5. *Excubiæ*, 6. constituuntur; & *Exploratores*, 7. emittuntur.

Excursiones, 8. fiunt Pabulationis & Prædæ causâ, ubi sæpius confligitur cum *Hostibus*, 9. velitando.

Tentorium summi *Imperatoris* est in medio *Castrorum*, 10.

The Army and the Fight. CXLI. Acies & Prœlium.

When the *Battel*

Quando *Pugna*

is to be fought the	committenda est,
Army is set in order, and	*Acies* instruitur, &
divided into the *Front*, 1.	dividitur in *Frontem*, 1.
the *Rere*, 2.	*Tergum*, 2.
and the *Wings*, 3.	& *Alas* (*Cornua*), 3.
The *Foot*, 4.	*Peditatus*, 4.
are intermixed	intermiscetur
with the *Horse*, 5.	*Equitatui*, 5.
That is divided	Ille distinguitur
into *Companies*,	in *Centurias*,
this into *Troops*.	hic in *Turmas*.
These carry *Banners*, 6.	Illæ in medio ferunt
those *Flags*, 7.	*Vexilla*, 6.
in the midst of them.	hæ *Labara*, 7.
Their Officers are,	Eorum Præfecti sunt,
Corporals, *Ensigns*,	*Decuriones*, *Signiferi*,
Lieutenants, *Captains*, 8.	*Vicarii*, *Centuriones*, 8.
Commanders of the Horse, 9.	*Magistri Equitum*, 9.
Lieutenant Colonels,	*Tribuni*,
Colonels,	*Chiliarchæ*,
and he that is the chief of	& summus omnium
all, the *General*.	*Imperator*.
The *Drummers*, 10.	*Tympanistæ*, 10.
and the *Drumslades*, 11.	& *Tympanotribæ*, 11.
as also the *Trumpeters*, 12.	ut & *Tubicines*, 12.
call to Arms,	vocant ad Arma
and inflame the Soldier.	& inflammant Militem.
At the first Onset	Primo Conflictu,
the *Muskets*, 13. and	*Bombardæ*, 13. &
Ordnance, 14. are shot off.	*Tormenta*, 14. exploduntur.
Afterwards they fight,	Postea pugnatur, 15.
15. hand to hand	cominus
with *Pikes* and *Swords*.	*Hastis* & *Gladiis*.
They that are overcome	*Victi*
are *slain*. 16.	*trucidantur*, 16.
or taken prisoners,	vel capiuntur,
or *run away*, 17.	vel *aufugiunt*, 17.
They that are for the Reserve, 18.	*Succenturiati*, 18.
come upon them	superveniunt

out of their *places where they lay in wait.*	ex *insidiis.*
The *Carriages*, 19. are plundered.	*Impedimenta*, 19. spoliantur.

The Sea-Fight. CXLII. Pugna Navalis.

A *Sea-fight* is terrible, when huge *Ships*, like *Castles*, run one upon another with their *Beaks*, 1. or shatter one another with their *Ordnance*, 2. and so being bored thorow they drink in their own Destruction, and are *sunk*, 3.	*Navale prœlium* terribile est, quum ingentes *Naves*, veluti *Arces*, concurrunt *Rostris*, 1. aut se invicem quassant *Tormentis*, 2. atque ita perforatæ, imbibunt perniciem suam & *submerguntur*, 3.
Or when they are set on fire and either by the firing of *Gun-powder*, 4.	Aut quum igne corripiuntur, & vel ex incendio *pulveris tormentarii*, 4.

men are blown up into the air, or are burnt in the midst of the waters,
or else leaping into the Sea are drowned.

A *Ship* that flieth away, 5. is overtaken
by those that *pursue her*, 6.
and is taken.

homines ejiciuntur in ærem, vel exuruntur in mediis aquis,
vel etiam desilientes in mare, suffocantur.

Navis fugitiva, 5.
intercipitur
ab *insequentibus*, 6.
& capitur.

CXLIII.

The Besieging of a City. Obsidium Urbis.

A *City* that
is like to endure a *Siege*,
is first summoned
by a *Trumpeter*, 1.
and persuaded to *yield*.

Urbs
passura *Obsidionem*,
primum provocatur
per *Tubicinem*, 1.
& invitatur ad *Depitionem*.

Which if it refuseth to do, it is assaulted by the Besiegers, and taken by storm.

Quod si abnuat facere, oppugnatur ab Obsidentibus & occupatur.

Either by climbing over the walls with *Scaling-ladders*, 2.

Vel muros per *Scalas*, 2. transcendendo,

or breaking them down
with *Battering-engins*, 3.
or demolishing them
with *great Guns*, 4.
or breaking through the
Gates with a *Petarr*, 5.
or casting *Granadoes*, 6.
out of *Mortar-pieces*, 7.
into the City,
by *Engineers*, 8.
(who lye behind
Leagure-baskets, 9.)
or overthrowing it with
Mines by *Pioneers*, 10.

They that are besieged
defend themselves
from the *Walls*, 11.
with fire and stones, &c.,
or *break out by force*, 12.

A *City*
that is taken by Storm
is plundered,
destroyed,
and sometimes laid even
with the ground.

aut diruendo
Arietibus, 3.
aut demoliendo
Tormentis, 4.
vel dirumpendo
portas *Exostra*, 5. vel
ejaculando *Globos Tormen-*
tarios, 6. e *Mortariis* (*balis-*
tis), 7. in Urbem
per *Balistarios*, 8.
(qui latitant post
Gerras, 9.)
vel subvertendo
Cuniculis per *Fossores*, 10.

Obsessi
defendunt se
de *Muris*, 11.
ignibus, lapidibus, &c.
aut *erumpunt*, 12.

Urbs
vi expugnata,
diriditur,
exciditur,
interdum equatur
solo.

Religion. CXLIV. Religio.

Godliness, 1.	*Pietas*, 1.
the Queen of Vertues,	Regina Virtutum
worshippeth God, 4. devout-	*colit Deum*, 4. humiliter,
ly, the Knowledge of God	Notitiâ Dei,
being drawn either from	haustâ vel ex
the *Book of Nature*, 2.	*Libro Naturæ*, 2.
(for the work commendeth	(nam opus commendat
the Work-master)	Artificem)
or from the	vel ex
Book of Scripture, 3.	*Libro Scripturæ*, 3.
she meditateth upon his	recolit
Commandments contained	Mandata ejus compre-
in the *Decalogue*, 5. and	hensa in *Decalogo*, 5.
treading Reason under	& conculcans Rationem,
foot, that *Barking Dog*, 6.	*oblatrantem Canem*, 6.
she giveth *Faith*, 7.	præbet *Fidem*, 7.
and assent	& assensum
to the Word of God,	Verbo Dei,
and *calleth* upon him, 8.	eumque *invocat*, 8. ut
as a Helper in adversity.	Opitulatorem in adversis.
Divine Services	*Officia Divina*

are done in the *Church*, 9.
in which are the *Quire*, 10.
with the *Altar*, 11.
the *Vestry*, 12.
the *Pulpit*, 13.
Seats, 14.
Galleries, 15.
and a *Font*, 16.

All men perceive that there is a God, but all men do not rightly know God.

Hence are divers *Religions* whereof IV. are reckoned yet as the chief.

fiunt in *Templo*, 9.
in quo est *Penetrale* (Adytum, 10.) cum *Altari*, 11.
Sacrarium, 12.
Suggestus, 13.
Subsellia, 14.
Ambones, 15.
& *Baptisterium*, 16.

Omnes homines sentiunt esse Deum, sed non omnes rectè nôrunt Deum.

Hinc diversæ *Religiones* quarum IV. numerantur adhuc primariæ.

Gentilism. CXLV. Gentilimus.

The *Gentiles* feigned to themselves near upon XIIM. *Deities*.

The chief of them were *Jupiter*, 1. *President*, and *petty-God of Heaven* ;

Gentiles finxerunt sibi prope XIIM. *Numina*.

Eorum præcipua erant *Jupiter*, 1. *Præses* & *Deaster cœli* ;

Neptune, 2. of the Sea;
Pluto, 3. of Hell;
Mars, 4. of War;
Apollo, 5. of Arts;
Mercury, 6. of Thieves,
Merchants,
and Eloquence;
Vulcan, (*Mulciber*)
of Fire and Smiths;
Æolus, of Winds:
and the most obscene of
all the rest, *Priapus*.

They had also
Womanly Deities:
such as were *Venus*, 7.
the Goddess of Loves,
and Pleasures, with
her little son *Cupid*, 8.
Minerva (*Pallas*), with
the nine *Muses of Arts*;
Juno, of Riches and Weddings; *Vesta*, of Chastity;
Ceres, of Corn;
Diana, of Hunting,
and Fortune;
and besides these *Morbona*,
and *Febris* her self.

The *Egyptians*,
instead of God
worshipped all sorts
of Beasts and Plants,
and whatsoever they saw
first in the morning.

The *Philistines* offered
to *Moloch*, 9. their Children
to be burnt alive,

The *Indians*, 10. even to
this day, worship the
Devil, 11.

Neptunus, 2. Maris;
Pluto, 3. Inferni;
Mars, 4. Belli;
Apollo, 5. Artium;
Mercurius, 6. Furum,
Mercatorum,
& Eloquentiæ;
Vulcanus (*Mulciber*),
Ignis & Fabrorum;
Æolus, Ventorum;
& obscænissimus,
Priapus.

Habuerant etiam
Muliebria Numina:
qualia fuerunt *Venus*, 7.
Dea Amorum,
& Voluptatum, cum
filiolo *Cupidine*, 8.
Minerva (*Pallas*), cum
novem *Musis Artium*;
Juno, Divitiarum & Nuptiarum; *Vesta*, Castitatis;
Ceres, Frumentorum;
Diana, Venationum;
& Fortuna:
quin & *Morbona*,
ac *Febris* ipsa.

Ægyptii,
pro Deo
colebant omne genus
Animalium & Plantarum,
& quicquid conspiciebantur primum mane.

Philistæi offerebant
Molocho (*Saturno*), 9. Infantes cremandos vivos.

Indi, 10. etiamnum
venerantur
Cacodæmona, 11.

Judaism. CXLVI. Judaismus.

Yet the true *Worship* of the true *God*, remained with the *Patriarchs*, who lived before and after the Flood.	Verus tamem *Cultus* veri *Dei*, remansit apud *Patriarchas*, qui vixerunt ante & post Diluvium.
Amongst these, that Seed of the Woman, the *Messias* of the World, was promised to *Abraham*, 1. the Founder of the *Jews*, the Father of them that believe: and he (being called away from the Gentiles) with his Posterity, being marked with the *Sacrament of Circumcision*, 2. made a peculiar people, and *Church* of God.	Inter hos, Semen illud Mulieris, *Messias* Mundi, promissus est *Abrahamo*. 1. Conditori *Judæorum*, Patri credentium: & ipse (avocatus a Gentilibus) cum Posteris, notatus *Sacramento Circumcisionis*, 2. constitutus singularis populus, & *Ecclesia* Dei.
Afterwards God gave his *Law*, written with his own Finger in *Tables of Stone*, 5. to this people	Postea Deus exhibuit *Legem* suam, scriptam Digito suo in *Tabulis Lapideis*, 5. huic Populo

by *Moses*, 3.	per *Mosen*, 3.
in Mount *Sinai*, 4.	in Monte *Sinai*, 4.
Furthermore, he ordained the eating the *Paschal Lamb*, 6. and *Sacrifices* to be offered upon an *Altar*, 7. by *Priests*, 8. and *Incense*, 9. and commanded a *Tabernacle*, 10. with the Ark of the Covenant, 11. to be made: and besides, a *brazen Serpent*, 12. to be set up against the biting of Serpents in the Wilderness.	Porrò ordinavit manducationem *Agni Paschalis*, 6. & *Sacrificia* offerenda in *Altari*, 7. per *Sacerdotes*, 8. & *Suffitus*, 9. & jussit *Tabernaculum*, 10. cum Arca Fœderis, 11. fieri: præterea, *æneum Serpentem*, 12. erigi contra morsum Serpentum in Deserto.
All which things were *Types* of the *Messias* to come, whom the *Jews* yet look for.	Quæ omnia *Typi* erant *Messiæ* venturi, quem *Judæi* adhuc expectant.

Christianity. CXLVII. Christianismus.

The only begotten eternal *Son of God*, 3.	Unigenitus æternus *Dei Filius*, 3.

being promised to
our first Parents in Paradise, at the last being conceived by the *Holy Ghost*, in the most Holy Womb of the *Virgin Mary*, 1. of the royal house of *David* and clad with humane flesh, came into the World at *Bethlehem* of *Judæa*, in the extream poverty of a *Stable*, 2.
in the fullness of time, *in the year of the world* 3970, but pure from all sin, and the name of *Jesus* was given him, which signifieth a *Saviour*.
When he was sprinkled with *holy Baptism*, 4. (the *Sacrament* of the *new Covenant*) by *John* his Forerunner, 5. in *Jordan*, the most sacred *Mystery* of the divine *Trinity*, appear'd by the *Father's* voice, 6. (whereby he testified that this was his *Son*) and the *Holy Ghost* in the shape of a *Dove*, 7. coming down from Heaven.

From that time, being the 30th year of his Age, unto the fourth year, he declared who he was, his words and works manifesting his Divinity, being neither owned, nor entertained by the *Jews*, because of his voluntary poverty.

promissus
Protoplastis in Paradiso, tandem conceptus per *Sanctum Spiritum* in sanctissimo utero *Virginis Mariæ*, 1.
de domo regiâ *Davidis*, & indutus humanâ carne, prodiit in mundum *Bethlehemæ Judæâ*, in summâ paupertate *Stabuli*, 2.
impleto tempore, *Anno Mundi* 3970, sed mundus ab omni peccato & nomen *Jesu* impositum fuit ei, quod significat *Salvatorem*.
Hic, cum imbueretur *sacro Baptismo*, 4. (*Sacramento novi Fœderis*) à *Johanne* præcursore suo, 5. in *Jordane* apparuit sacratissimum *Mysterium* Divinæ *Trinitatis*, *Patris* voce, 6. (quâ testabatur hunc esse *Filium* suum) & *Spiritu sancto* in specie *Columbæ*, 7. delabente cœlitus.

Ab eo tempore, tricesimo anno ætatis suæ, usque an annum quartum, declaravit quis esset, verbis & operibus præ se ferentibus Divinitatem, nec agnitus, nec acceptus a *Judæis*, ob voluntariam pauperatem.

He was at last taken by these (when he had first instituted the *Mystical Supper*, 8. *of his Body and Blood* for a Seal of the *new Covenant* and the remembrance of himself) carried to the *Judgment-seat of Pilate*, Governour under *Cæsar*, accused and condemned as an innocent *Lamb*; and being fastned upon a *Cross*, 9. *he dyed*, being sacrificed upon the Altar for the sins of the World.

But when he had revived by his Divine Power, he rose again the third day out of the *Grave*, 10. and forty days after being taken up from *Mount Olivet*, 11, into *Heaven*, 12. and returning thither whence he came, he vanished as it were, while the *Apostles*, 13. gazed upon him, to whom he sent his *Holy Spirit*, 14. from *Heaven*, the tenth day after his *Ascension*, and them, (being filled with his power) into the World to preach of him; being henceforth to come again to the *last Judgment*, sitting in the mean time

Captus tandem ab his (quum prius instituisset *Cœnam Mysticam*, 8. *Corporis* & *Sanguinis sui*, in Sigillum *novi Fœderis*, & sui recordationem) raptus ad *Tribunal Pilati*, Præfecti *Cæsarei*, accusatus & damnatus est *Agnus* innocentissimus; actusque in *Crucem*, 9. *mortem subiit*, immolatus in arâ pro peccatis mundi.

Sed quum revixisset Divinâ suâ Virtute, resurrexit tertia die è *Sepulchro*, 10. & post dies XL. sublatus de *Monte Oliveti*, 11. in *Cœlum*, 12. & eo rediens unde venerat, quasi evanuit, *Apostolis*, 13. aspectantibus, quibus misit *Spiritum Sanctum*, 14. de *Cœlo*, decima die post *Ascensum*, ipsos vero, (hac virtute impletos) in Mundum prædicaturos; olim rediturus ad *Judicium extremum*, interea sedens

at the *right hand*
of the Father,
and interceding for us.
From this *Christ* we
are called *Christians*, and
are saved in him alone.

ad *dextram*
Patris,
& intercedens pro nobis.
Ab hoc *Christo*
dicimur *Christiani*,
inque eo solo salvamur.

Mahometism. CXLVIII. Mahometismus.

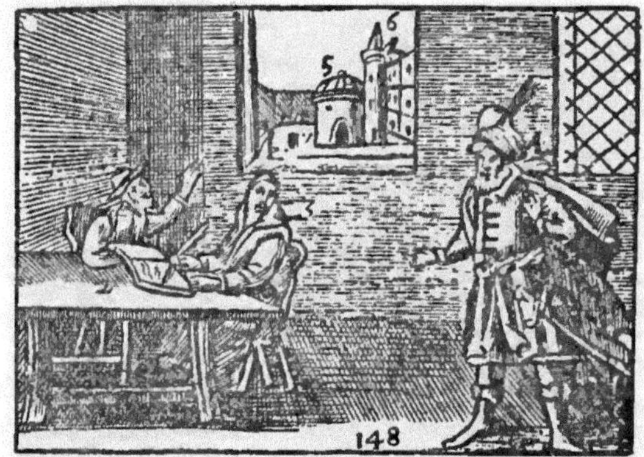

Mahomet, 1.
a warlike Man,
invented to himself
a new Religion,
mixed with *Judaism*,
Christianity and *Gentilism*,
by the advice of a *Jew*, 2.
and an *Arian Monk*, 3.
named *Sergius*; feigning,
whilst he had the *Fit of*
the Falling-sickness,
that the *Archangel Gabriel*
and the *Holy Ghost*,
talked with him,

Mahomet, 1.
Homo bellator,
excogitabat sibi
novam Religionem,
mixtam ex *Judaismo*,
Christianismo & *Gentilismo*,
consilio *Judæi*, 2.
& *Monachi Ariani*, 3.
nomine *Sergii*; fingens,
dum laboraret *Epilepsia*,
Archangelum Gabrielem,
& *Spiritum Sanctum*,
secum colloqui,

using a *Pigeon*, 4.
to fetch Meat
out of his Ear.
His *Followers*
refrain themselves
from *Wine;*
are circumcised,
have many *Wives ;*
build *Chapels*, 5.
from the *Steeples* whereof,
they are called to Holy
Service not by *Bells*,
but by a *Priest*, 6. they
wash themselves often, 7.
they deny the *Holy Trinity:*
they *honour Christ*,
not as the *Son of God*,
but as a great *Prophet*,
yet less than *Mahomet ;*
they call their *Law*,
the *Alchoran.*

adsuefaciens *Columbam*, 4.
petere Escam
ex Aure sua.
Asseclæ ejus
abstinent se
à *Vino ;*
circumciduntur,
sunt *Polygami ;*
exstruunt *Sacella*, 5.
de quorum *Turriculis*,
convocantur ad sacra
non a *Campanis*,
sed a *Sacerdote*, 6.
sæpius se abluunt, 7.
negant *SS. Trinitatem :*
Christum honorant,
non ut *Dei Filium*,
sed ut magnum *Prophetam*,
minorem tamen *Mahomete;*
Legem suam vocant
Alcoran.

Gods Providence. CXLIX. Providentia Dei.

Mens States | Humanæ Sortes

are not to be attributed	non tribuendæ sunt
to *Fortune* or *Chance*,	*Fortunæ* aut *Casui*,
or the *Influence of the Stars*,	aut *Influxui Siderum*,
(*Comets*, 1.	(*Cometæ*, 1.
indeed are wont to por-	quidem solent nihil boni
tend no good)	portendere)
but to the provident	sed provido
Eye of God, 2.	*Dei Oculo*, 2.
and to his *governing Hand*,	& ejusdem *Manui rectrici*, 3.
3. even our *Sights*,	etiam nostræ *Prudentiæ*,
or *Oversights*,	vel *Imprudentiæ*,
or even our *Faults*.	vel etiam *Noxæ*.
God hath his *Ministers*	*Deus* habet *Ministros*
and *Angels*, 4.	suos, & *Angelos*, 4.
who accompany a *Man*, 5.	qui associant se *Homini*, 5.
from his birth,	à nativitate ejus,
as *Guardians*,	ut *Custodes*,
against wicked *Spirits*,	contra malignos *Spiritus*,
or the *Devil*, 6.	seu *Diabolum*, 6.
who every minute	qui minutatim
layeth wait for him,	struit insidias ei,
to tempt	ad tentandum
and vex him.	vel vexandum.
Wo to the mad	Væ dementibus
Wizzards and *Witches*	*Magis* & *Lamiis*
who give themselves to	qui Cacodæmoni se
the *Devil*,	dedunt
(being inclosed in a *Cir-*	(inclusi *Circulo*, 7.
cle, 7. calling upon him	eum advocantes
with Charms)	Incantamentis)
they dally with him,	cum eo colludunt
and fall from God!	& à Deo deficiunt!
for they shall receive their	nam cum illo
reward with him.	mercedem accipient.

The Last Judgment. CL. Judicium extremum.

For the *last day*
shall come
which shall raise up the
Dead. 2. with the sound of
a *Trumpet*, 1. and summon
the *Quick* with them
to the *Judgment-seat*
of *Christ Jesus*, 3.
(appearing in the Clouds)
to give an Account
of all things done.

When the *Godly* & *Elect*, 4.
shall enter into life eternal into the place of Bliss,
and the new *Hierusalem*, 5.

But the *Wicked*
and the *damned*, 6.
shall be thrust into *Hell*, 8.
with the *Devils*, 7. to be
there tormented for ever.

Nam *dies novissima*
veniet,
quæ resuscitabit *Mortuos*, 2. voce *Tubæ*, 1.
& citabit *Vivos*,
cum illis
ad *Tribunal*
Jesu Christi, 3.
(apparentis in Nubibus)
ad reddendam rationem
omnium actorum.

Ubi *pii* (*justi*) & *Electi*, 4.
introibunt in vitam æternam, in locum Beatitudinis
& novum *Hierosolymam*, 5.

Impii vero.
& *damnati*, 6.
cum *Cacodæmonibus*, 7. in
Gehennum, 8. detrudentur,
ibi cruciandi æternum.

The Close. CLI. Clausula.

Thus thou hast seen in short, all things that can be shewed, and hast learned the *chief Words* of the *English* and *Latin Tongue.*	Ita vidisti summatím res omnes quæ poterunt ostendi, & didicisti *Voces primarias Anglicæ* & *Latinæ Linguæ.*
Go on now and read other good *Books* diligently, and thou shalt become *learned*, *wise*, and *godly.*	Perge nunc & lege diligenter alias bonos *Libros*, ut fias *doctus*, *sapiens*, & *pius.*
Remember these things; fear God, and call upon him, that he may bestow upon thee the *Spirit of Wisdom.*	Memento horum; Deum time, & invoca eum, ut largiatur tibi *Spiritum Sapientiæ.*
Farewell.	Vale.

L.

M.

N.

O.

P.

Q.

R.

An Index of the Titles.

C.

D.

E.

F.

G.

H.

Trinuni Deo Gloria.

FINIS.

Lightning Source UK Ltd.
Milton Keynes UK
UKHW010123200522
403255UK00002B/342